Mature monogamy is both crucible and sanctuary. In it, love, awareness, passion, and integrity function as one, generating an intimacy that truly *transforms*.

TRANSFORMATION THROUGH INTIMACY

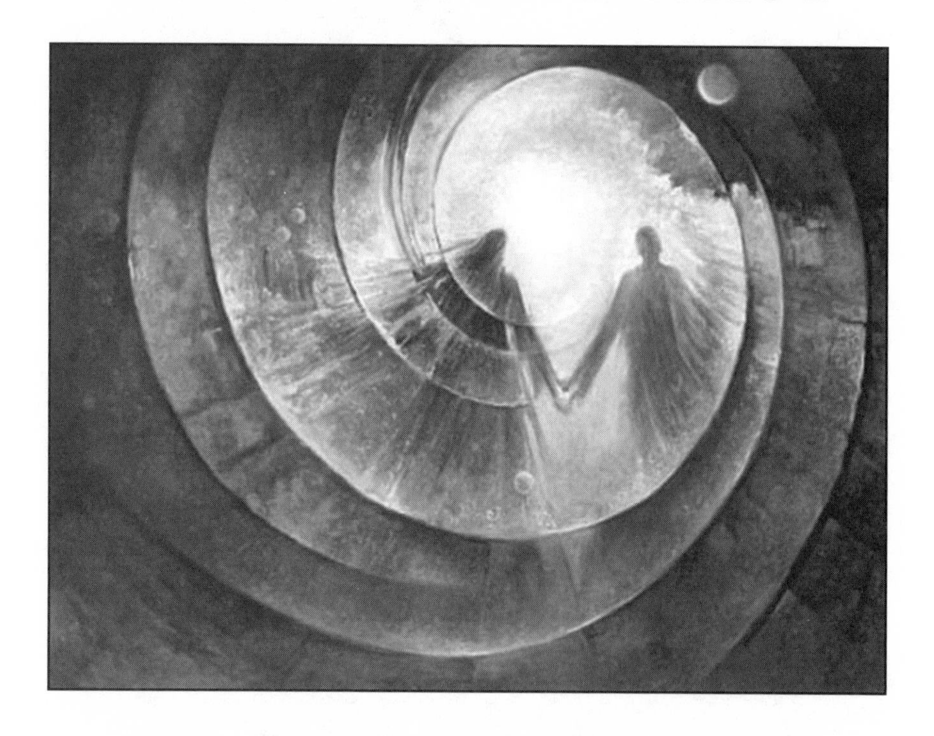

THE JOURNEY TOWARD MATURE MONOGAMY

Robert Augustus Masters

TEHMENOS PRESS

Tehmenos Press

For more information, visit
www.RobertMasters.com

ISBN: 978-0-9737526-5-6

Printed in the United States

ALSO BY ROBERT AUGUSTUS MASTERS

Darkness Shining Wild:
An Odyssey to the Heart of Hell & Beyond
Meditations on Sanity, Suffering, Spirituality & Liberation

Freedom Doesn't Mind Its Chains
Revisioning Sex, Body, Emotion & Spirituality

The Anatomy & Evolution of Anger
An Integral Exploration

Divine Dynamite (revised edition)
Entering Awakening's Heartland

CONTENTS

For Diane

My wife, truest friend, ever-deeper beloved, and partner in all things, without whom this book could not have been written.

My solo travels are done
Our shared heart my sun
As we together die
Into the undying One
Without forgetting
The broken many
No matter what my chains
I'll love you until only love remains

The passage from immature to mature monogamy is not just a journey of ripening intimacy with a beloved other, but also a journey into and through zones of ourselves that may be quite difficult to navigate, let alone get intimate with and integrate with the rest of our being.

But however much this passage might ask of us, it gives back even more, transforming us until we are established in the unshakable love, profound passion, and radically intimate mutuality that epitomize mature monogamy. And even if we don't end up in such a relationship, our having taken the journey toward it will immeasurably benefit us in whatever we do.

Introduction

THE EVOLUTION OF INTIMATE RELATIONSHIP

Intimate relationship is, to put it mildly, at a very interesting point in contemporary culture.

In a small but significantly increasing percentage of the population, intimate relationship has over the last four or five decades evolved so far from its long-established ways — mutating in diverse directions — that its very nature and structuring, once such an unquestioned given, is clearly up for some deep questioning and reformulating.

Reformulating, revisioning, restructuring, reinventing — how we tend to look at intimate relationship is changing almost as rapidly as intimate relationship itself.

One result of this is that many of us do not have a particularly clear view of intimate relationship. We look, but usually don't bother to look inside our looking, being so caught up in checking our rearview mirrors or getting nostalgic for the future that we don't see all that much of what's right before of us. Nonetheless, we have to admit that *something* is different about intimate relationship now. We look back just two generations, and it seems as if we're looking back many hundreds of years. Things are moving that fast.

For a very long time, intimate relationship was viewed and lived, with few exceptions, as an alternative — and not necessarily an equivalent alternative — to spiritual life. There was the householder, and there was the spiritual seeker, and there wasn't much overlap between them. As wide as this split was for men, it was even wider for women. Intimate relationship was something you did — or endured — until there was cultural permission to do something "deeper."

Now there not only is a significant amount — small by conventional standards, but still substantial enough to register on the radar screens of cultural evolution — of permission (cultural and otherwise) for something "deeper" to happen *within* intimate relationship, but also an increasing pull toward it. So intimate relationship has, at its leading edge, become less a prelude to spiritual opening and awakening, and more a crucible *for* it.

This is nothing less than great news. Grounding our transpersonal/spiritual dimensions in the raw stuff of daily life (enroute to integrating all that we are) — as is so amply supplied by intimate relationship and its everyday dynamics — is much needed, especially with regard to the increasingly precarious positioning we as a species are occupying. Spirituality directly lived in the context of ordinary life is spirituality that can have a real impact on the quality of life — staying plugged into our spirituality *during* our relationship's bumpier times provides us with a much needed perspective, greatly increasing the odds that we won't sweat over what's not worth sweating over. Daily life — and intimate relationship in particular — can be contemporary culture's ashram.

If we can access our spirituality — and access it at a deeper level than that of belief — during the inevitable trials and challenges of intimate relationship, we can probably access it just about anywhere.

Intimate relationship as a crucible for awakening from the entrapping dreams that we habitually animate — sounds good, doesn't it? But once our honeymoon with this is over, the real labor begins. The path is not neatly laid out for us, in part because we, through our very relatedness with our intimate other, are *cocreating* that path, that relational unfolding, as we go, feeling our way — more often than not on our hands and knees — toward what really matters. In this, we travel together not only through adventures high and low, but also, as we will see, take up residence in deeper stages of intimate relatedness.

These are exciting — excitingly alive and excitingly unstable — times for intimate relationship. The playing field for men and women has, in far more ways than not, been leveled, making possible encounters and openings not generally available when women were second-class citizens or worse, cut off from their own voice and power. Now men and women have far more of an opportunity to meet eye to eye, belly to belly, heart to heart, without the disempowering ethics of earlier times. A meeting of true partners no longer has to be such a rarity.

However, a level playing field is not without its own perils, for it's easy to reduce it to a flatland of force-fed equality. Once that women had more rights and a more inclusive cultural context in which to live, they began leaving men, in trickles at first, then in droves — which brought more and more men to psychotherapy or at least to their knees — and men then began to realize that they would have to do more than flash some bucks, be nice for a while, or raise a fist to keep women with them. Many relationships became arenas of negotiation, wherein equality between the partners did not liberate, but rather only fed the status quo.

Neurotic egalitarianism seized the helm, declaring an across-the-board equality that not only increased comfort, but simultaneously deadened. The husband typically depicted on television sitcoms — sexless, inept, and supremely unattractive — reflected and reinforced the notion that for men marriage was, whatever its trappings, a *trap*. And so on.

Intimate relationship shifted for many from barbaric to bland, infecting more than a few with nostalgia for the barbaric, because at least that had some juice, especially for the men. Affairs multiplied. Pornography infiltrated the mainstream, attracting refugees from the wastelands of conventional marriage.

There had — and very much needed — to be a move away from the banal stagnation and plastic tedium of such conventionality, but it mostly went backward instead of forward, while often acting as if it were indeed moving forward (as exemplified by multiple-partnering practices and their accompanying rationalizations). Monogamy itself started to take some heat, getting overassociated with the deadening of passion.

Nevertheless, amidst all this relational upheaval there was something else starting to emerge, something neither barbaric nor bland, something at once deeply passionate, caring, awakened, and rooted in integrity and love — a stage of intimate relationship that I call *mature monogamy*. The practice and living of mature monogamy is at the heart of this book. Much will be said about how to move through the territory between immature monogamy and mature monogamy. That territory, that ever-shifting yet ever-fertile zone of potential relational evolution, features a remarkably rich mix of landscapes, emotional and otherwise, and can seem overwhelming in its complexity and overlapping concerns.

And so, as an orientation/travelling aid, I have throughout this book explored most of the topics through the lenses of four stages of intimate relationship — me-centered, we-centered codependent, we-centered coindependent, and being-centered — which I'll introduce after saying a bit about stages.

There are stages to intimate relationship, just as there are stages — to take but two examples — to cognitive and moral development. A stage exists not as an organic entity or thing unto itself, but rather as a cohesive, nontransient, stably established assembly or "structure" of coexisting qualities. We don't so much directly experience stages as *arrive* at them (though we do experience firsthand the various qualities that constitute them), at some point recognizing through a variety of signs, behavioral and otherwise, that we have arrived at a particular stage.

This is simpler than it might sound. There is, for example, plenty to an egocentric stage of morality — huge amounts of developmental research and conjecture having been invested in considering it — but most of us easily grasp what it actually means to be at this stage of moral development. The same applies to a prerational cognitive stage as compared to a rational cognitive stage, and so on. What follows is not *the* stage model for intimate relationship, but simply the model that makes the most sense to me, based both on my own experience (especially with my wife Diane) and on all the work I have done with couples.

The first stage is *me-centered relationship*. This is an ego-run arrangement, with the egoity of one partner usually dominating that of the other. Each partner's credo, however well camouflaged, basically is: "What's in it for me?" Some may appear to be more selfish, more full of themselves, but others, perhaps nicer or more passive, are still obeying — however indirectly — a what's-in-it-for-me dynamic, if only to ensure or reinforce their security.

Not surprisingly, the dominant member is usually male, although that has started to shift somewhat in the last few decades. So we basically have two egos — two cults of one — in some sort of coalition, however uneasily governed. There's not much ongoing intimacy here, but there may nonetheless still be times of profound connectedness, union, and love — that is, elevated *states* — the presence of which may create the illusion that the couple is doing better than is actually the case.

In me-centered relationship, there is not much intimacy with the various factors that together make up the relationship. We might, for example, know next to nothing about our anger (its signs of arising, its originating factors, its behavioral manifestations, and so on), even though we are frequently angry. By contrast, in a truly intimate relationship, intimacy is cultivated with each partner's anger — and also with every other aspect of the relationship — as well as with the relationship as a whole.

Monogamy at this stage is immature, held in place through a power dynamic rooted mainly in fear and obedience (often featuring the man holding most of the power). Non-monogamous urges are only superficially curbed, and are, whether acted-out or not, often indulged (this ordinarily being far more characteristic of the man than the woman). Betrayal of the relationship, whether through sexual or emotional affairs or pornographic obsession, is common.

The next stage is *we-centered codependent relationship*. It is not without me-centered tendencies — for each stage not only transcends the previous stage, but also *includes* it, however peripherally or slightly — but is not so readily run by them. Here, equality is not only valued, but often is *overvalued*, so that differences tend to get flattened or drained of life. The couple is now not so much two cults of one in coalition, as one cult of two over against the rest of life.

This is not always be as isolated as it sounds, for the membrane around the couple may be somewhat permeable, but there still is a strongly guarded separation from whatever exists outside their coupledom. Within their self-contained world, they negotiate over what would seemingly best serve their relationship — they are important, but their relationship is more important. It is their security, their sanctum, their bubble of immunity, and whatever might threaten it from within is defused, diplomatically and otherwise.

Monogamy at this stage is also immature, held in place by a power dynamic rooted in exaggerated or force-fed tolerance (generally shared equally by both partners). Non-monogamous urges are generally curbed, muted, or repressed, at best being only vicariously indulged. Outright betrayal of the relationship is uncommon; the betrayal that does occur is mostly a betrayal of the potential of each partner for the sake of the safety and comfort provided by their relationship.

The third stage is *we-centered coindependent relationship*. Here, both partners make a priority out of maintaining their individuality, while also remaining, at least to a minor degree, a cult of two. Negotiation over differences is still commonplace, but there are more interpersonal risks taken. Tolerance is not so rigidly enforced. Autonomy, though much more adult here than in me-centered relationships, is often given too much weight. There usually is insufficient vulnerability between the partners. And though there is more passion here than in we-centered codependent relationship, it is not usually permitted full expression. Promiscuous urges are usually neither indulged (as in the first stage) nor suppressed (as in the second stage), but rather are exposed and discussed in a way that mostly does not significantly threaten the relationship.

Monogamy here is starting to shed its immaturity; there is some sense of a deeper kind of relationship, with some steps toward that perhaps being taken. What needs to be surrendered at this stage is each partner's overattachment to autonomy and aversion to deep communion (which they tend to associate with romanticism or neurotic fusion).

The fourth stage is *being-centered relationship*. Although it knows itself to be above/beyond the previous three stages, it does not look down upon them (doing so would be a first-stage habit), and does not even want to, for it chooses intimacy with *all* its qualities, however dark or immature or unappealing, and it recognizes that all of the qualities that characterize early stages of relational intimacy are, to whatever degree, *part* of it. Rather than just transcending these qualities, being-centered relationship also cultivates *intimacy* with them, so that they are not only included in it, but are also known from the deep inside. (Thus do we relate not *from* our neuroses, but rather *to* them.)

Monogamy at this stage is mature, possessing an integrity that's firmly rooted in shared love, shared power, shared depth, shared presence. Non-monogamous urges present no problem, because they have all but ceased to exist; there is simply no interest in them (at the same time, however, there is great, ever-deepening passion). Betrayal also has ceased to exist, the very seeds of it having no soil from which to sprout.

Monogamy now is not a choice, but a profoundly obvious and sacred *given*. Finding freedom *through intimacy* is a living reality at this stage, consistently and naturally and fully participated in by both partners, because they have reached the point where there is no real alternative to doing so.

For those in being-centered relationships, the limitations of monogamy are not entrapping, but *liberating*.

At the far reaches of mature monogamy, relationship enters such a depth of intimacy that that which is beyond all relatedness consistently infuses the relationship. This does not mean the end of the relationship, but rather only a further grounding of it in Being.

Mature monogamy may sound wonderful, but how do we get there? After all, we can't just read about it and then go live it. Much has to be done before mature monogamy is significantly available to us. For starters, we need to expose, face, and directly work — and not just cognitively! — with whatever is immature in us. We can't, for example, remain emotionally illiterate or morally stunted if we want to be in a truly intimate relationship.

Much of this book therefore concerns what needs to be explored and done in order to prepare us for mature monogamy. The passage from immature to mature monogamy is not just a journey of ripening intimacy with a beloved other, but also a journey into and through zones of ourselves that may be very difficult to navigate, let alone get intimate with and integrate with the rest of our being.

The longing for a being-centered relationship, the aching for mature monogamy and passionately awakened partnership with our beloved, is our primary guide when it is openly felt, providing incentive and inspiration for exploring places and patterns in ourselves that we otherwise would likely avoid or only marginally visit.

And it is into these places and patterns, these areas of darkness, pain, and heavy wounding, that we must go, if we are to be truly ready for mature monogamy. This is not some kind of romanticized or paint-by-numbers shadow-work, but rather an odyssey that, asking everything of us, readies us for a life *big enough* to include mature monogamy.

In short, moving toward mature monogamy matures us.

Part of the problem in writing about intimate relationship is that it loses much of its aliveness and visceral authenticity when chopped up into categories. So I will not be as neat as perhaps I could be in my structuring of this book, letting the contents of its chapters mingle and overlap some. (Some of the chapters may seem familiar to readers of my other books, as they've been taken from these and modified to fit this book.) Each aspect of an intimate relationship affects and is affected, however indirectly, by every other aspect of the same relationship; this book will resonate, as best it can, with much the same interactive, intersubjective spirit.

Mature monogamy, if it is genuinely mature, does not look down upon immature monogamy, but instead cultivates intimacy with its qualities, however lowly, dense, or dark those may be. Everything has its place. Egocentric impulses, for example, are not banished or subjected to spiritual ambition's ego-eradicating programs, but rather are approached with sufficient depth and clarity to divest them of any power to threaten or otherwise undermine our relationship, leaving them — like the rest of our "lower" qualities — as no more than colorful, functionally peripheral threadings that simply enrich the weave of our relationship.

So, in the spirit of intimacy with all that we are, including knowing that we'll be aligned with our heart's deepest longing when we stop avoiding the work that needs to be done, I invite you to explore with me the anatomy, evolution, and transformational power of intimate relationship, with a special focus on mature monogamy.

White Rock, British Columbia

July 25, 2007

This edgeless depth we share
This fluid mutuality so bare
This meeting nothing can delay
This quick-kindling ecstasy
Leaving us bonelessly asway
In love's everwild eternity
We trade the slightest glance
And our flesh starts to dance
Sweet sweet electricity
Such sublime simplicity
Touching the one through the two
Meeting beyond what we thought we knew
Your delight in my newly shaved head
And in how I worded what I just said
My delight in your vocal bouquets
And in the familiar deep of your gaze
Is but part of a very long list
That began long before we first kissed

The more we blend
The more we don't end
The more we hold what's dying
The more we are held by what's divine
Expanding to include each other
Our only shared name that of lover

I the husband of your heart
You the wife of mine
Long have we been apart
Now begins our time
Bound together yet free
Twin flames of intimacy

I. Getting Oriented

Chapter One

IMMATURE & MATURE MONOGAMY

Monogamy is not doing so well these days, and probably was not doing much better in earlier times, regardless of lower (or even nonexistent) divorce rates and other appearances to the contrary. Many longtime monogamous couples (especially we-centered codependent couples) have remained together more for reasons of security and comfort than real intimacy. A substantial number of couples have not had sex with each other (or, most of the time, with anyone else) for a long stretch (and we may be talking *years*), and many of those who are still having sex with each other aren't enjoying it all that much. And it's not just sex that's gone stale or flat, but the very bond itself, which could probably be more accurately described as *bondage*, regardless of its coziness.

More often than not, monogamy operates much like a cult of two, mired in a mutual pact not to rock the boat, while trying to find some pleasure amidst its stagnant or tepid waters. A mirage of intimacy greened by oases of distraction and occasional bursts of closeness. Quite understandably, various alternatives to monogamy have found a receptive audience in the last four or five decades (and I'm talking here about contemporary culture — plenty of older cultures have been characterized by forms of relationship other than monogamy).

So is monogamy really on its way out? No, and not just because it is so culturally entrenched and still held up by most as the best way to form a lasting love partnership. What *needs* to go — and what at last appears ready to go — is *not* monogamy, but rather monogamy as it usually is practiced. In what follows, I'll clarify this by comparing conventional monogamy with what it could be. And to further flesh things out, I will also bring in polyamory (relationship with more than one partner at a time), because of its connection, however shadowed or marginal, with everyday monogamy.

If we were to put monogamy up against polyamory, with regard to depth, awakening potential, and capacity for real intimacy, which would come out on top? Monogamy, by a landslide, so long as we're talking about *mature monogamy*, as opposed to conventional (or growth-stunting and passion-dulling) monogamy, referred to from now on as immature monogamy.

Immature monogamy is, especially in men, frequently infected with promiscuous desire and fantasy, however much that might be repressed or camouflaged with upstanding virtues. Airbrush this, infuse it with talk of integrity and unconditional love and jealously-transcending ethics, consider bringing in another partner or two, and you're closer than near to polyamorous or multiple-partnering territory.

At this point, those promoting multiple-partnering might jump in and say that it is not immature monogamy, because of how loving and open it is. Though there may in some cases be *some* truth in this, it glosses over the difficulties associated with such "love" and "openness." One such difficulty is the restriction that multiple-partnering (or so-called "open relationship") places on attachment, coupled with its denial that it is doing so. If we have more than one lover, then when things get rocky with one, we can just go to another, instead of staying with and working with that rockiness; thus can we keep ourselves removed from getting as attached as we might if we were to be with only *one* deep intimate.

Another difficulty has to do with the fuzzy or easily-collapsed boundaries that often accompany the enthused "openness" of "open" relationships (this of course also often characterizes immature monogamy), through which the *eroticizing* of unresolved issues (like craving being wanted or craving being in control) is confused with sexual freedom. The charge we have with what is unresolved in us is simply that, an *excitation* (whether positive or negative) or energetic intensity rooted in our reaction to various events from our past; when we reroute this excitation into the pleasuring possibilities of sex, we are literally moving away from the pain that underlies such excitation, the pain that, when consciously entered and illuminated, can liberate us (for more on this, see Chapter 23).

Immature monogamy gets neurotically attached, multiple-partnering generally avoids (and is a distraction from) attachment, and mature monogamy permits attachment, but without making a problem out of it. And what's so important about attachment in intimate relationship? Well, for starters, without it we are not nearly vulnerable enough in our relationships; it's easy to be loving but not vulnerable, but without sufficient vulnerability, we won't open — and be broken open — to the depths of relational intimacy of which we are capable. (More will be said later about the role of attachment in intimate relationship.)

Those caught up in — or dragged down by — immature monogamy are going to want some compensation for their doing time in the cult of two that is immature monogamy, and high on that list, especially for men, is erotic pleasure. If they are not sexually happy with their wives, which is very often the case, then they're probably going to end up hanging out with or acting out their pornographic leanings, which may include polyamorous fantasies. They have not yet learned that eroticism (excessive interest in sexual promise and opportunity) promises happiness, but real sex *begins* with happiness (for more on this, see Chapter 21).

Men in general are not naturally monogamous (at least compared to women), and typically feel as though they are losing something — usually their "freedom" — through settling into monogamous relationship. Conjugal entrapment this seems to be, feebly saluted by those who, having already done plenty of time there, are still "tied down" — no wonder there are so many jokes about marriage's power to emasculate! It's no accident that sexy husbands who have eyes only for their wives are all but an extinct species in television and film.

Monogamy simply won't work for men (or for women) until they move toward its mature form. How? By waking up and committing themselves to continuing to wake up, especially when in the midst of immature monogamy's neurotic rituals and compensatory erotic fantasies.

Immature monogamy is, however, not entirely useless, because time spent in it can — through the sheer dissatisfaction and disappointment that it generates — ready us for something deeper and far more fulfilling that nevertheless still is monogamous.

Mature monogamy is a life-enhancing, passion-enriching, spiritually-deepening choice, and it's a choice which we cannot truly make until we've become incapable of immature monogamy and unseducible by multiple-partnering's advances. At this point, we can love so deeply and so fully in a one-on-one relationship that we can become profoundly attached — not addicted, but *attached* — so that if our beloved were to suddenly die or betray us, our heart would be ripped wide open.

Consciously opening ourselves to such attachment means that we are not going to run away or dissociate from whatever pain our relationship might bring us. Here, we are not repressing our multiple-partnering urges, but have instead simply outgrown them, leaving ourselves no escape routes (such as another lover or some other potent distraction) from our chosen relationship.

Mature monogamy is all about finding freedom *through* intimacy, especially the profound and singular intimacy that characterizes a truly bonded partnership. Our relationship with our beloved is then a sacred container which we are deeply committed to taking good care of and protecting. This means, among other things, not leaking energy elsewhere (especially erotically), not distracting ourselves from challenges and difficulties in the relationship, not indulging in reactivity and negativity, and not putting any limit on our love for our beloved.

Such deep focus, such devotion to our shared depth, such shared safety to get vulnerable and *really* alive with each other, such shared emotional and existential and spiritual nakedness, is an ongoing choice made all the richer by cutting off all exits. Then she is not just a woman to him, but *all* women and Woman Incarnate, and he is to her not just a man, but *all* men, and Man Incarnate. This is not metaphysical mush, but a living reality, full-blooded and more often than not ecstatic.

Having said all this, I'm not condemning multiple-partnering, but simply attempting to place it in a relational context that divests it of any glamor with which we might want to associate it. Multiple-partnering confuses love and sexuality; yes, we can love more than one person deeply, but this does not mean that we can or need to be sexual with them! Putting a limit on whom we are sexual with does not necessarily put a limit on whom we are loving deeply! Those committed to mature monogamy find freedom through limitation.

Those who have not yet entered mature monogamy are, however unwittingly or subtly, generally going to be chronically on the verge of betraying their partner (and not just sexually). In the sexuality of immature monogamy, fantasy usually plays a big role, allowing us to pump energy into mindgames that make pleasurable sensation and release more important than true intimacy. Erotic consolation. If we are busy fantasizing during sex, our partner is reduced to little more than a prop in our masturbatory drama.

But in the sexuality of mature monogamy, fantasy is all but nonexistent (being utterly unnecessary), since the living reality and succulent mystery of each other is more than enough to keep both joyously and effortlessly turned on, especially given the remarkably deep shared *trust* that is present. Such trust is rooted in the dynamic safety and integrity inherent to mature monogamy; it is a safe place to let go of playing it safe, inviting us into the adventure of awakening through relationship.

Immature monogamy may be an avoidance of overt multiple-partnering, but multiple-partnering is an avoidance of mature monogamy. Put another way, immature monogamy and multiple-partnering are two aspects of a stage of relatedness that must be outgrown before mature monogamy can take the stage.

One more thing about mature monogamy: It makes possible the kind of relationship that can transcend relationship. Touching the One through the two. Freedom through intimacy. Mature monogamy is, in other words, *a liberating bondage*, a deeply joined freefall into What-Really-Matters. Multiple-partnering is too wrapped up in the payoffs of the shallow end of the pool to generate the depth possible through mature monogamy.

In mature monogamy, there is not room for another lover, but more than enough room for the Beloved.

Regarding immature monogamy and the territory between it and mature monogamy: Jump in, wherever you are. When you hit bottom, push off and surface, then paddle out a bit deeper. Eventually, you will leave the arms of the familiar, and have no bottom to hit, no end to love, no limit to depth. This is the beginning of mature monogamy.

Your face a landscape
My eyes love to wander
Your gaze an oasis
For my gypsy ways
I've done time in many places
Running out of land
With nowhere to stand

Hold me soft and hold me deep
Wrap your skin around me

Your face a familiar mystery
My hands and eyes know by heart
Your deeply swooning electric flesh
Effortlessly entangled with mine
Bursting with a radiance
That's awareness and love
Functioning as one

Your face an impossibly eloquent territory
I have committed to memory
Your naked recognition
All the welcome I need
My solo travels are done
Our shared heart my sun
As we together die
Into the undying One
Without forgetting
The broken many

Chapter Two

RADICAL INTIMACY

When single people ask me how they can live a deeper life, I often suggest that they get into an intimate relationship — and *really* get into it — because it likely will, among other things, catalyze the surfacing and exposure of just about everything they would rather avoid — which is precisely what they need to stop avoiding!

And not only does intimate relationship help in bringing the less-than-flattering aspects of both partners to the surface — that is, into a position where they can be clearly seen and worked with — but also can provide a remarkably conducive environment for dealing, and dealing thoroughly, with such things.

Intimate relationship has immense transformational possibility when we approach its difficulties — and approach them with more than just our intellects! — as opportunities instead of as problems. Opportunities for what? To know ourselves more deeply, to love and live more fully, to become intimate with *all* that we are — in short, to be freed from our suffering. Freedom through intimacy.

In a truly intimate relationship, we learn to find freedom not from limitation, but *through* limitation.

As was described in the Introduction, there are stages to intimate relationship: me-centered, codependent we-centered, coindependent we-centered, and being-centered. Although there is some overlap between these stages, they are nonetheless distinct from each other. The fact that various *states* (emotions, moods, times of confusion or clarity, and so on) can show up in all four stages may seem to complicate things, unless we clearly distinguish between states and stages. (Chapter Four considers this in more depth.)

States, whether high or low, dark or light, numinous or hellish, are very transient phenomena, appearing at all developmental levels, but stages are far more stable, existing as psychophysical structures that tend to remain in place once established. For example, the cognitive stage of formal reasoning, reached by most in their early teens, does not disappear once established, despite being submerged or replaced from time to time by less-than-rational states.

Those who are firmly established in being-centered intimacy do not lose their relational maturity, regardless of the intrusion of various states. They may briefly behave immaturely from time to time, but this does not remove them from their being-centered closeness, at least for any significant length.

Effectively working with states — acknowledging them, openly facing them, giving them suitable expression, and, especially, relating *to* rather than *from* them — is essential to any couple's well-being.

This means becoming intimate with our states — and also with those of our partner — so that we can approach them not with aversion, but with curiosity and openness. Instead of two centers of reactivity squaring off (the me-centered), or overcompromising (the codependent we-centered), or keeping too much distance (the coindependent we-centered), we have two centers of mutual responsiveness together facing, and compassionately facing, the reactivity of both. Chapter Seven examines this is in detail, as do many other upcoming chapters.

Now let's take a more intimate look at intimacy.

Intimacy, derived from the Latin *intimus* (meaning "innermost") has a number of meanings, probably the most common of which is that denoting relational closeness. It can also signify "close" in the sense of intrinsic or essential, particularly with regard to our deepest nature. Closely related to this is the use of "intimate" to suggest something of a very personal or private nature. Other meanings include the assurance of an informal warmth (as in an "intimate" setting), and the presence of sexual activity in a relationship (as in "they are intimately involved"). Intimacy can also mean familiarity with a particular subject.

What the various meanings of intimacy have in common is the notion of closeness, in more than just a juxtapositional sense. In intimacy, there is a deliberate involvement with an "other" (which could be a person, an object, or a state) that transcends mere proximity, since that "other" is permitted to enter the "circle" of one's self.

How close we can actually get to the "other" depends upon more than the degree of inclusion, however; indiscriminately throwing open our borders invites not intimacy, but rather exploitation, delusion, and regret. A certain separation from the other may be needed, if only to bring that one into clearer focus. Without such separation, intimacy becomes little more than fusion, exaggerated cohesion, a cult of two, a "we" estranged both from "I" and the collective "us" of humanity. Incorporating spiritual practices into intimate relationship may still not be enough — it's easy to let our embrace of our intrinsic non-separateness separate us from our differences!

In genuine intimacy, togetherness and apartness coexist, each honoring, illuminating, and embracing the other, as if in acknowledgment of the fact that they actually are fundamentally inseparable — as was stated in the last chapter, we cannot separate unless we are already connected, and we cannot connect unless we are already separated. Such is the *apparent* paradox of relationship.

In becoming intimate with *all* that we are — and therefore with all that is — we more and more deeply recognize who and what we are. Instead of trying to get rid of what we don't like about ourselves, we instead relate to it in such a way that it no longer obstructs our well-being. That is, we *choose* relationship with our every quality — and I mean "our" in both a singular and collective sense — rather than separation. Intimacy then becomes more our passion than does transcendence, and relationship becomes not something to outgrow, but rather something to fully embody and live, especially as we realize, right to our core, that everything — everything! — exists *through* relationship.

Through wholehearted, wide-awake participation in committed relational intimacy, we enter the One (or our innate inseparability) — and therefore also the Many — through the two, finding through our relationship with our beloved the Beloved in all things, so that the very details of daily life, however mundane or tedious, become an obvious and always present awakening path, ever inviting us into a deeper life, a life of full-blooded awakening, love, integrity, and joy.

This means no more turning away from ourselves, so that we are in a position to cultivate intimacy with our every disowned, excommunicated, neglected, shunned, or otherwise rejected piece of self, rather than just homesteading in — and trying to make the best of — a divided selfhood.

Without the ground of real intimacy with the "less-than-spiritual" or unwanted dimensions of ourselves, the sky that opens for us will only be the ceiling of our hungriest thought.

To be intimate with all things is to let all things serve — catalyze, further, reinforce, stabilize — our awakening from the entrapping dreams and assumptions we habitually animate and occupy.

And what better place to practice intimacy than in the depths of fully committed intimate relationship?

Chapter Three

WHAT'S RIGHT ABOUT WHAT'S WRONG IN RELATIONSHIPS

Intimate relationship promises much, but only delivers what we put into it. We need to ask not only what we want from such relationship, but also what we are willing to do to manifest that. Wanting to be cocooned or secured through relationship is very different than wanting to be healed, awakened and deepened through relationship. If we really want the latter, we need to open to what it will — and has to — ask of us, knowing that it won't necessarily be an easy ride, at least not until we are stably established at a being-centered stage of relationship.

Of course, if it were easy, we surely would have done it long ago. But, as we shall see, it is the very difficulties that arise as we more deeply enter relationship which provide most of the raw material for reaching the depth and ease of relationship for which we yearn.

We want so damn badly to *really* get it right in our relationships, as is so exhaustively demonstrated by all the books and television shows about how to have better relationships, all the songs of heartache and break and mend, all the hunting and hoping and groping for that special somebody who'll do right by us, all the efforting, manipulation, self-marketing, and strategizing to get it right, to get it to last, to get it to really satisfy — all of it sentenced to the labor of making us feel better or at least more sure or secure, consuming more of our attention and energy than we'd bargained for, leaving us burdened and bewildered and close to not much more than depression and burnout, yet still hot-wired to enough paint-by-numbers relationships advice to be marooned from the fact that real relationships, relationships rooted in love and a mutual commitment to waking up, are not only less nice and more challenging than we thought, but also more messy (like this sentence).

Before it becomes being-centered, intimate relationship sometimes can be such a drag, such a high maintenance hassle, such a drain, knocking us around until we swear that we'll not reenter such a hazardous arena, regardless of its feel-good payoffs. But it usually doesn't take much time for us to jump back in again, high on hope (as when we get a tidbit of unexpected openness from an emotionally stingy partner). Maybe we will do better this time; maybe we'll meet someone who will treat us better; maybe we won't be so intolerant; maybe we won't be so tolerant; maybe we'll not let ourselves be fooled; maybe we'll handle things better; and so on. Such endlessly rich and — more often than not — melodramatic material this is for standup comedy, soap operas, and everyday gossip. And for something deeper, too, as we shall see.

Sloppy dialogue, emotional illiteracy, go-nowhere arguments, little cruelties, everyday stupidities, mismatched desires, mechanical rituals, halfheartedness, putting off what needs to be done — these are some of the things that clutter me-centered and we-centered relationships. They resist the vacuuming of good intentions. They resist both rational persuasion and emotional pleas. They go wherever we go, following us into and out of our dreams. At essence, however, they are just longtime habits tracking mud and worse into our shared space, while masquerading as us. If left undealt-with, this leaves our lives debilitatingly messy, no matter how well-scrubbed our place and face is.

But in the messiness-*including* integrity and vitality of being-centered relationship (as epitomized by mature monogamy), such habits become nakedly obvious, clashing and colluding with each other before a *mutually* knowing eye, clearly needing more than a laundry spin, more than a communications course, more than better table manners. Such habits have gotten away with referring to themselves as us, but now cannot do so for long, as we, more and more, learn to relate *to*, rather than *from*, them.

Intimate relationship not only includes the mingling and encounter of differences, but also, sooner or later (mostly in me-centered and we-centered bonds), catalyzes a blatant exaggeration or flaring-up of differences, a vividly dramatized exposure — however unwittingly animated! — of various oppositions, impasses, difficult mixes, and overdefended positionings that would have otherwise more than likely remained more camouflaged or untouched.

As unpleasant as this might feel — and the worse it feels, the more valuable it likely is — it signals a great opportunity to know ourselves more fully, because so much of what needs to be worked through for our own maturation is right before us, literally outfront and in our face, inviting us, for starters, to openly face it.

Intimate relationship thus provides an environment, both outer and inner, wherein what we do not like or do not want to know — or simply do not know — about ourselves is given center stage, just like in a dream. And there we may stand or stumble, seemingly transfixed by the spotlight, held in place both by our attachment to the other and to our own ideologies, feeling the heat of our preferences starting to flame into reactivity.

And this point, where we'd typically (if primarily in me-centered or we-centered relationships) just trot out our usual roles — the misunderstood one, the victim, the reasonable one, etcetera — is precisely where even a *trace* of wakefulness is of immense use, to inwardly acknowledge not only our state, but also our degree of *identification* with that state. When a *mutually* compassionate eye can be cast upon the highlighted reactivity of one or both partners, the relationship is on course.

The more deeply we dive, the less we mind upsetting waves, finding within intimate relationship an increasingly compelling invitation to find freedom through our shared heart, our shared body, our shared limitations, our shared boundlessness, our shared mortality, our shared yes, our shared being, our shared all...

But as good as it gets, intimate relationship at me-centered and we-centered stages still can be a two-headed hell-raiser. There are times when the shared heart is split into two densely-walled camps; there are times when the shared body is a vacant lump; there are times when the shared limitations are just a royal pain in the shared ass; there are times when the shared boundlessness is just an idea; there are times when the shared mortality is but a tenured deadening; there are times when the shared being is crowded with loneliness; there are times when the shared yes is riddled with doubt. The good news is that such times are fierce teachers, testers and potential deepeners of our faith, inviting us to get back on track.

When we are intimate with another, we can be very, very hurt. We can become crazily jealous, possessive, obsessed, angry in ways we never thought possible, our spiritual practices shredding into near nonexistence in the storms of our pain and reactivity. It might seem under such conditions that our capacity for awakening has been severely diminished, but that is from the viewpoint that sees only the turbulence, the chaos, the unpleasantness of what is happening. However, in such rough and wild waters swirls another possibility, one equipped with nothing but a lifeline to our heartland. If we take hold of it, we start to recognize what's right about what's wrong; we treat the shit as compost; we let the pain tear open our heart; we learn to love when we are not being loved or don't feel loved, and to give what we ache to be given.

However, if we only try to *think* our way through our relationship hassles, we merely confine their turbulent forces in our minds, thereby intensifying our confusion, instead of letting such forces fuel our leap into a more fitting level of being, recognizing and treating relational intimacy not as an end, but rather as a means, an extremely potent crucible for awakening's alchemy.

When we stop caring so much about who's right, we find enough heart to recognize what's right about what's wrong, allowing ourselves to be more comfortable with the uncomfortable, including the fear of being so close and connected that even a small unkindness from our partner cuts us. This is not about being oversensitive, but *vulnerable.* A relationship that lacks vulnerability is a relationship sentenced to the shallows.

We do, however, need to be careful about our possible egoic investment in having a "deep" relationship — there is nothing like an intimate relationship to let us know that we're not as developed as we may have thought!

We might, in meditative retreat or metaphysical flight, assume without much challenge that we are indeed sitting with our less-than-admirable qualities, being mindful of them, and so on, but real relationship does not waste much time in letting us know the difference between sitting *with* such qualities and sitting *on* them.

Entering such relationship is generally a rude awakening. It steps on the toes of our egoity, unimpressed by our credentials, drawing us into an evolutionary drama in which our neuroses initially get to star as us, and then are divested of such pretension, becoming but grist for the mill of awakening. To the degree that we are attached to our egoity and neurotic rituals, a relationship will, more often than not, seem like just one insult after another, prior to becoming being-centered.

The sooner we ask what's right about what's wrong in our relationships, the sooner we'll discover the real value and purpose of them.

This may mean approaching our relationship in ways to which we are not accustomed. Sometimes being off our path is our path. Sometimes what works best is to spend some time in what doesn't work (this, however, does *not* mean we should be tolerant of abuse!). For example, watching the worst of television, as an alternative to meditation too rigidly adhered to, can be good medicine for spiritual constipation. We can get so busy trying to be good, trying to stay on the path, trying to be a successful somebody in a conscious relationship, that we stagnate, barely able to move beneath the sheer weight of all our documented failures.

Making discerning room for our intimate relationship to sometimes be somewhat messy — which does *not* mean making a virtue out of laziness, inconsiderateness, and mean-spiritedness! — helps keep it clean, undirtied by purity and the tyrannies of psychosocial correctness.

This does not, however, necessarily mean clear sailing. Any relationship can trigger us. Good relationships trigger the hell out of us without trashing the relationship; great relationships trigger the hell out of us while deepening the relationship. And the best relationships use whatever happens, however difficult or disheartening, not only to deepen the relationship, but also to awaken us beyond it.

What does not work in a relationship (assuming that neither partner is abusing the other), is what can make it truly work — especially in the sense of giving us sufficient jolts to alert us to our trances, consensual and otherwise — but *only if* such difficulties are dealt with by *both* partners not as problems, but as opportunities. Not easy, not easy at all. After all, this asks that we venture from the shoreline into some really big waves. We might then strengthen or more firmly anchor our bond with our partner; or we might finally see that we are not right for each other, no matter what we do; or we might start new practices together; or we might recognize that the depth of our love will sustain us through all, or that it is not enough to keep us together; and so on. No guarantees.

We may think it would be great to be at our edge — which is where growth primarily occurs — but actually being there is not necessarily much of a picnic. In fact, it sometimes may be so unpleasant, so scary, so hard to stomach or handle, that we find some convincing alibis to do otherwise — such as literally leaving the relationship, withdrawing from it while still in it, or keeping it relatively superficial.

About leaving a relationship: There is no inherent virtue in staying; what matters is that we don't leave prematurely. Hanging in there when it's rough or unnourishing is just as important as *leaving* when it's been rough or unnourishing for *too long*. Many of us have stayed too long in relationships, convincing ourselves that we *should*, regardless of our partner's behavior, stay and try to make wise use of whatever happens to us — *anything* other than leaving!

Sometimes the most loving thing we can do for another is to leave them, especially when they refuse to work on themselves or acknowlege their part in whatever relational difficulties are arising. We have to ask ourselves — and not when we are reactive! — if we are *truly* being served or furthered by the relationship: Are the difficulties therein challenging us in a way that we need to be challenged, or are they simply eroding us? If the answer to this varies according to our mood, it's not the answer.

We can't connect unless we are already separate; and we can't separate unless we are already connected. Such is the apparent paradox of relationship. Real intimacy is the art of balancing togetherness and apartness, so that they are not so much polar opposites as they are dance partners. The relationship is the dancefloor; what we don't like about each other and ourselves the wallflowers; and the music and movement Life itself, at once outlasting us and appearing *as* us.

In the liberating bondage of real intimacy, our separateness is not a problem, but rather a ticket to real freedom, providing more than enough dissatisfaction and disillusionment to push us toward what we *really* need.

Part of what makes a relationship truly rewarding is an ongoing mutual intimacy with what doesn't work in the relationship, however small that might be.

The obstacles we encounter in relationship are not really obstacles, but catalysts in drag. Catalysts for what? For waking up. Be grateful to have someone so close to you who can so easily push your buttons — and maybe even install a few! It's not so easy to remain buttoned-up when we're in close to another. Healthy relationships don't let us remain intact, cool, immune. They kick our mutual butt with such fierce compassion that we can't sit for long on our stuff. How infuriating, how inconvenient, what a pain in the ass! And what a gift. (And what ease, once we have entered being-centered relationship, wherein fierce compassion is needed only occasionally.)

And what a wonderfully sobering and illuminating joy — to enter so deeply into shared living that *everything* is permitted to awaken us. And to be so close, so attached, so deeply bonded that we cannot get away for very long from the inevitable challenges of such relationship.

This is freedom, freedom *through* limitation, freedom through traveling together no matter what the weather.

Freedom through intimacy.

Chapter Four

STATES & STAGES IN THE EVOLUTION OF RELATIONSHIP

It is crucial for the well-being and evolution of our intimate relationship that the difference between states and stages be, and remain, clear.

States — or experiential arisings or conditions which tend to *occupy* us for their brief stay — are very transient (moods being but one example), whereas stages — or developmental structures/levels — are closer to being permanent or stably established, much like long-held traits. *States pass from us* (no matter how often they may return), but *we pass from stages* (unless of course we stop evolving).

Dreaming, irritation, sadness, equanimity, paranoia, ecstasy, reactivity, confusion — these are all states, compellingly real usually only while they last. When they pass, other states make their entrance, snagging our attention and infusing us with their certainties. And, to complicate things, states and stages are frequently confused, especially when a state sticks around for longer than normal (chronic depression being a common example). Prerational cognition, rational cognition, egocentric morality, ethnocentric morality — these can manifest as states, but also are actual stages (of cognition and morality), not flitting in and out of existence, but rather staying put, at least until they are outgrown.

So states come and go in a relatively short time, finding expression through whatever stage we may be at. States can appear at any stage of relationship (me-centered, we-centered, being-centered), easily creating the illusion, in the case of "higher" states, that a couple is further along than is actually the case.

For example, an experience of boundary-dissolving, ecstatic unity with our partner suddenly happens (and not necessarily only through sex), shaking us to our core, and we then frame/interpret that experience and its afterglow according to our prevailing sense of reality, which can range from from self-serving romanticism ("This means that you are meant to stay with me") to fundamentalist fervor ("This means that our way is the only way") to all-serving gratitude ("May everyone experience this"). It all depends on where we're at developmentally.

So our undeniably unitive experience might simply be used to reinforce our egocentric orientation, if that's from where we *primarily* function. Then we, paradoxically, are actually using our experience of profound connectedness to keep ourselves disconnected from the rest of life. Those in an abusive relationship may use the arising of such states to justify the relationship's continuation as it is. Even violent relationships can have sublime times. By contrast, if we are living mostly from a being-centered perspective, then our unitive experience will simply be extended, however indirectly, to all beings, not because we think it's a good idea, but because that's from where we are primarily functioning.

Another example: We are angry at our partner, so angry that we get reactive, letting our anger mutate into aggression; what we say and do here is all but automatic. The word "react" says it all: to *re*-act. It's pre-scripted, and we're caught up in its predictable momentum, swept along by our righteousness. Sound familiar? It happens to all of us, no matter how evolved we may take ourselves to be. In short, we've gotten ourselves into a state. Quite a state. Now, what do we *do* with it? This depends on how we interpret and treat it. If we're primarily operating from an egocentric perspective, we'll just go ahead and let fly, not questioning our reactivity unless perhaps it is met with enough force to shake us out of our trance.

However, if we're mostly we-centered, then we'll, at least to some degree, recognize our reactivity as something harmful to our relationship, even as we let it proceed. Such recognition acts as a braking force here, so that we are less likely to stay with our reactivity for as long as we would if we were mainly me-centered. Our concern for our us-ness, our cocreated intersubjectivity, our relatedness, keeps some wakefulness operating while we are busy being reactive.

And if we are mostly being-centered, our reactivity usually does not get very far, for it is almost always seen for what it is right from its initial arisings, and so is not allowed to build up much steam. Here we relate *to* it, rather *from* it. That is, we are no longer *identified* with it. We then do not try to get rid of our reactivity, but instead simply cultivate a relationship with it that keeps it in its place. (For more on this, see Chapter Eight.)

Interpretation — including of states — is stage-determined and stage-bound. (Not until we can clearly recognize that we tend to see things not so much as they are but as *we* are, can we be truly responsible in our relationships.)

We may — out of ambition, spiritual and otherwise — try to impose on ourselves an interpretive framework that is mostly out of our reach, thus burdening ourselves with shoulds, as our actual, real-time interpretive framework continues, whether behind the scenes or not. Intellectually considering more "advanced" or more radically inclusive interpretive frameworks is *not* the same as directly experiencing and living and truly "getting" such frameworks!

We may read about a particular frame of reference favored by those who are apparently highly developed or evolved, and even feel a certain pull toward it, but because we are not *living* it (and therefore are not significantly aligned with it), we cannot truly appreciate it — we are then like tourists taking pictures of a building, having not only little or no sense of what is inside it, but also not having the ability to actually get inside it. (And even if we do somehow get inside it — as perhaps catalyzed through an extreme or at-the-edge experience, such as a violent shock or a great loss or a near-death experience — we will not be able to stay long enough to get much out of it.)

Recognizing the stage we are at means, in part, having some intimacy with the various "lines" of development — especially the cognitive and moral. The cognitive line progresses from prerational to rational to postrational and beyond; the moral line from egocentric (me) to ethnocentric (a narrow or tribal we) to worldcentric (the collective we of humanity) and beyond. The various lines are not truly separate from each other, interacting in all kinds of ways, but it nonetheless can be useful to view them as separate entities, especially when they are not operating in parallel. For example, we might be at a relatively advanced stage cognitively, but be far behind morally. We may have a high IQ (intellectual intelligence), but a low EQ (emotional intelligence). And vice versa.

In me-centered relationships, there is unillumined confusion between states and stages; in we-centered relationships, there is less confusion, the differences being recognized to some extent, but usually only intellectually; and in being-centered relationships, there is little or no confusion between states and stages.

In getting intimate with a state, we start seeing it more clearly. We get close enough to familiarize ourselves with its properties and signs, while keeping enough distance to be able to bring it into clear focus. In this, we are simultaneously experiencing that state and existing beyond it.

Being intimate with stages, however, is not so easy, since a stage is not so much an experience as a prevailing *condition*. States are to weather as stages are to climate.

Where a state is an arising, a stage is an arrival. Where states get to us, we get to stages.

We can develop intimacy with stages we've passed beyond (for example, it's not difficult for rationality to clearly see and discerningly include prerationality), but intimacy with the stage which we're at is more difficult, to the degree that we're identified with it — and intimacy with stages beyond us is not possible, though the illusion that this is possible may be created through intimacy with *states* that are ordinarily beyond us.

We may also sometimes so often be in (or be in close proximity to being in) "higher" states that we don't question our *stage* of development. For example, a spiritual teacher may frequently be — or at least appear to be! — in exalted meditative states, but nonetheless still mostly operate from a much grosser place — his *actual* stage of development — the rest of the time, while using his exalted times to reframe his sloppy or abusive behavior as something spiritual or beyond reproach (which may be reinforced by those around him choosing to view all that he does as divinely inspired). Such behavior is quite common in intimate relationship. For example, we may trot out our good points, perhaps righteously listing them in emphatic detail, right after we have behaved badly toward our partner and won't openly admit it.

And we must not become too literal in considering stages; they are not necessarily as neatly ordered or stacked as it might appear. We are not just at one stage (whether cognitively, morally, spiritually, or otherwise), but are also, however peripherally, at *all* of those "below" the one we predominantly inhabit. Being-centered morality is big enough to include me-centered morality, but not vice versa.

Also, it's crucial to recognize that the "above" and "below" of stages is *not* an elitist structuring! Some might project hierarchical tyrannies onto the very mention of "higher" stages, but "higher" here does not necessarily mean better, but rather only points to an undeniable and unavoidable *positioning* — rationality, for example, possesses more perspective than prerationality, simply because it is in a position to "see" more.

As we truly are, we include it all.

Beyond every state and stage, here we are — and when we cultivate this perspective, we become, to whatever degree, capable of taking good care of our every state, while allowing our evolution — personal, relational, and beyond — to follow its natural course, stage after stage.

When we are capable of recognizing a state as a state, feeling it fully without allowing its viewpoint to be our viewpoint, we are already in mature monogamy's domain, *listening* closely and consciously not only to whatever state we are in, but also to that out of which it arose.

Which brings us to our next chapter...

Chapter Five

THE ART OF LISTENING

He is speaking slowly and carefully, accurately describing the verbal dynamics of what has just happened between himself and his partner. Several times she starts to speak, but he gently waves her off, saying that when he's done, she'll have her turn to speak. On he goes, deftly dissecting the tiny argument they'd gotten into five or so minutes ago.

She leans toward him, her eyes sad, her jaw tightening, as if fighting to hold back her speech; she is afraid that if she interrupts him, he will very likely label her as immature, or — though he'd never say it outloud — as a bitch. So she keeps quiet. Two more minutes pass. He's still not done.

Finally, she breaks eye contact, looking down. He shows no sign of noticing. She's thinking about leaving him, and he doesn't have a clue. The signs are there, and have been for a while, but he's missing them. When he stops a minute later, she has nothing to say. Tears cover her face. They never argue again. Such brilliant cognition, such an incisive, finely nuanced mind, but such emotional retardation — this is what she writes about him, a few months after she has left him.

Listening is an art.

It asks for more than open ears, more than data-absorbing focus, and much more than agreement or disagreement. Full attention, undivided attention, wide-awake attention, attention that is not allowed to wander or shrink, is essential to listening, especially in the context of intimate relationship.

Although listening might seem like a passive activity — hence the commonplace framing of the listener as lesser than the speaker in many a masculine mind — it is actually quite *dynamic*. Its requisite openness is not an undiscerning or weakly-boundaried receptivity, but rather a vital clearing for deep hearing.

Listening is all about being wholly attentive to our partner, and not just to what is being said! As we hear what isn't being said, and respond to that without speaking, we deepen our resonance with our partner, becoming an open space for the fullest possible expression of what he or she is attempting to convey to us.

As we listen so fully and with such authentic *interest* that our own thoughts all but disappear, we can hear our intuition's messages loud and clear, without any dilution of the attention which we are giving to our partner. The deeper that we take this — or the deeper that we allow it *to take us* — the richer and more obviously multidimensional the intersubjective (or "we") space between us and our partner.

When the flow of words ceases, don't be too quick to break the silence. Sometimes silence has a lot to say, without any need for translation. Listening together to silence — silence being far more than the absence of sound! — can be a very rewarding practice to share.

Listening requires not only full attentiveness, but also care and patience. If others do not *feel* our caring for them while we're listening to them, they probably will be less likely to speak freely to us. If they do not feel our patience — our unstrained yet dynamic waiting, our awakened surrender to making haste slowly — they usually will be less likely to take whatever time they need to say what must be said.

When we are *really* listening, we are not only receiving our partner's words, pauses, somatic messages, emotional state, and corresponding energies, but are also providing them with a conducive space in which to express themselves, level upon level.

We then learn to listen not only to their *interiority* (their perceptions, feelings, thoughts, and so on) and to their *exteriority* (their body language, behavior, and so on), but also to the qualities of the intersubjective space between them and us — as well as to the familial, cultural, and planetary forces which may be influencing them. The point is not to split these up into neat categories — for they all coexist simultaneously and share considerable overlap — but to make sure that we are covering all the bases as best we can as we listen, ever letting our listening deepen.

For those in me-centered relationships, there is ordinarily not much listening. Each is so busy with his or her own concerns that there is very little room to *really* hear what the other is saying, or trying to say. Most of what does get through is framed in terms of what it can or can't do for us. Here, we mostly listen to the imperatives and siren call of our own conditioning, with little or no awareness that we are doing so. And even when we do really listen, it's usually not for long, as our interest easily wanders away.

For the we-centered codependent relationship, there's more listening, but there's not much depth to it. If we sense that what we are hearing may not do much for our relationship, we tend to turn a deaf ear to it. We argue less than those in me-centered relationships, but nevertheless still make agreement and disagreement the most important elements in dealing with conflict; this means that when we are listening, we usually don't let ourselves really listen to what our partner is feeling, but rather get overfocused on the *content* of what they are saying, placing it all in an arena of negotiation. Thus do we keep our listening superficial — civil, perhaps, domesticated, very likely, but not very deep.

For we-centered coindependent relationships, things are generally much the same. Our listening is mostly in the service of our remaining autonomously intact, and so we tend to filter out whatever might obstruct or challenge that. Agreement and disagreement remain of paramount importance to us, with the result that we give the nonverbal dimensions of our partner's sharing not much of a hearing, except to the degree that it preserves our relationship and our independence within it. Only in the maturing of this stage, as our need for autonomy and our need for intimate communion come more into balance, do we start really listening to our partner.

For the being-centered relationship, listening is a *given*.

It is not a should, nor a duty, but rather an utterly natural, intimacy-enhancing practice. Both partners enjoy, and *consistently* enjoy, listening to each other. Conversation is almost always easy, and listening almost always effortless. Agreement and disagreement are, with minimal fuss, kept peripheral to openly felt resonance and mutuality; both partners usually can, with ease, stand apart from their need to be right, viewing it with self-illuminating care. Passionate expression is not avoided; both listen to the other, no matter what their state is (and no matter how intensely it may be expressed), and clearly *want* to do so.

Listening can get very deep here; psychic attunement is common, with both often knowing what the other one is about to say, to the point where it's no longer amazing, but just the way things are. In a sense, partners here are, when in each other's company, almost always listening to each other, on more levels than meet the eye and ear.

So how to work with all this?

Let's start with the me-centered couple, imagining that they are in the presence of a suitably skilled psychotherapist, which of course presumes that they have some interest in dealing with their difficulties. We can also, as we read this, let ourselves more fully feel what is me-centered in us, as well as in our relationship.

First of all, in our hypothetical psychotherapy session there is very little point, at least initially, in actually pointing out the characteristics of listening at each stage of relationship. It's not time to pull out any maps, other than *very* simple, nonthreatening ones, like those that clearly distinguish between surface and depth, open and closed, abusive and nonabusive, attentive and non-attentive.

This can — and needs to — be presented in a way that does not reinforce shame; after all, surface and depth (as well as open and closed, abusive and nonabusive, and so on) are signifiers which apply to an enormous variety of situations. Making sure that the couple understands the difference between surface and depth (as well as between open and closed, abusive and nonabusive, and so on) in relationship is usually an easy (and gracefully evolving) undertaking, both creating some rapport and *introducing* the bare rudiments of listening.

A short — and I mean *short* — talk about the importance of listening might follow. If one member of the couple, after having heard this, interrupts the other without any admission of having done so, such behavior will be quickly pointed out, with the added suggestion that the interrupter practice not interrupting the other for the rest of the session. And on it goes. Once things get heavier, with reactivity and accusations showing up, a more overtly in-charge presence is needed to keep the session on track. Now what is being listened to is not just language, but also feeling.

Let's now temporarily leave the therapy chambers and see what might happen when the couple is at home, with no one else around. Probably a lot of reactivity, with both quoting the therapist as backing them up. At best, they might notice if they are being listened to, or if they actually *are* listening; even a moment or two of this can be very helpful. They might also notice, however fleetingly, their investment in being in power, or being right, or being on top — or perhaps the opposite.

Now back to the therapy room: This may be a good time to teach some very basic mindfulness. One person might be practicing breath awareness, for example, while the other is delivering their usual repertoire of complaints and accusations. During this, the therapist can keep the meditative one on track, so that the other's reactivity does not so easily get under their skin. Gradually, in this and other ways, the reactivity of both is exposed in as *non-shaming* a manner as possible, so that it becomes, however slowly, an *object* of awareness. Each learns not only to listen more closely to the other, but also to themselves. As they do so, they start to enter the territory of we-centered (and, in embryonic form, being-centered) relatedness.

Those in we-centered codependent relationship usually have some listening skills, but most of the time these are kept in the service of the compromise-based let's-not-rock-the-boat nature of their relationship. Going deeper here is not easy, for the couple is likely dug in, holed up in their pseudo-sanctuary of negotiated comforts. But because they are not fully alive in their relationship — diplomacy can, after all, be very deadening — and have an investment in remaining like this, more depth will be probably be difficult to access. Getting them to listen to *themselves* is as much a challenge as getting them to listen to the deeper needs of their partner.

However, as soon as each hears the other's need for more depth and openness, and hears the lack of such depth and openness not as their fault but for what it *actually* is, progress can be made. As they leave the "safety" of their codependent connection, fear will usually arise, but sooner or later so too will excitement, perhaps accompanied by the insight that most fear is just excitement in drag.

Some couples may be so addicted, however, to their compromises and dug-in security, that movement is all but impossible. For them, all that can be done — and it's no small thing! — is to help them see what they are doing and what is possible, and leave them to make their choices based upon this.

Couples in we-centered coindependent relationships are usually easier to work with, mostly because they have more commitment to taking care of themselves. Getting them to listen to themselves is not the challenge; getting them to listen to the deeper needs of their partner is.

Their overattachment to autonomy must be slowly but surely dismantled, while taking into account the unaccustomed vulnerability they will feel as they shift into a deeper interdependence.

What they must learn to do is expand their circle of self to include, and fully include, each other. Such expansion will really stretch their boundaries; any rigidity here will be experienced as pain, pain that must be entered into until it releases its grip and allows a psychoemotional elasticity.

Initially, couples at this stage will say they don't want to surrender their freedom; later, they will realize that what needs to be surrendered is not their freedom, but rather their *entrapment* in their so-called freedom.

"Freedom through intimacy" will at first just be a concept to them, perhaps interesting, but not much more. Later — as they listen more closely to what is actually going on in their relationship — it will not be a concept, but a living reality and opportunity, an invitation to enter a deeper life.

And what about listening in being-centered relationships? It is utterly *natural.* Listening is not engaged in now and then, but almost always. The mind of the one listening is ordinarily quite quiet, uncluttered with thoughts, not kicking into activity until it is time to speak. Agreement or disagreement with what the other is saying is kept peripheral to feeling, directly and deeply feeling, what the other is saying. There is an unforced, steady empathic resonance that makes communication very easy most of the time. Even when there is discord, as when anger arises, the communication continues and its discordant elements are given room to speak up, without, however, being allowed to run the show.

What helps keep things on course when things get rough or messy is the radically deep trust between the two. If one tells the other that he or she is not listening, listening usually occurs very quickly. There's no power struggle here, no battle for dominance, so both members of the couple have no investment in winning; in fact, the whole drama of winning and losing, of being overrun or defeated, does not get any stage time.

There is no need to do practices to get back on track; being aware of being off track provides more than enough impetus to get back on track, and quickly.

Listen. What do you hear? Now listen even more closely. Sometime in sessions, following very deep work, when clients are digesting what's happened, I have them close their eyes, do an awareness practice for a few minutes, and then listen to the silence (my therapy/group room is *very* quiet) for a bit, perhaps also letting themselves *feel* its presence, both all around and inside them.

Listening to silence is not the same as listening to the mere absence of sound. Listen. Silence just said something. Don't lose it in the translation. Silence *does* speak.

Listening is undividedly attentive, dynamic receptivity, as respectful as it is empathetic.

Listen until there is no self-contained listener, no self-conscious center of hearing, but only listening. And don't forget to listen while you are speaking; listening to our listener only deepens our connection. Listen. There's so much being said to you, through you, by you, for you, as you, at this very moment...

Chapter Six

KEEPING IN TOUCH WHEN WE'RE OUT OF TOUCH

The closer we are to our intimate other, the more painful the absence of closeness between us.

A feeling of disconnection arises and thickens, the mind makes lists of reasons why, and attention gauges the density and strength of the distance between us. Something in us says "oh shit!" or "why?" and something else in us says "this too" — voices of alarm and voices of acceptance, simultaneously ricocheting through us.

Some witnessing capacity is present, but love is having trouble taking root (unless we're established in a being-centered relationship). Stormwinds of endarkened feeling make it difficult. And attachment to being right makes it even more difficult.

What's left of us cannot see a way out (except perhaps intellectually), but there is a knowingness, without thinking, that the way out is *in*. Instead of turning away from our pain, we can turn *toward* it.

Being close to our partner feels so good, so heartwarming and enlivening, that it's easy to make a problem out of times when we don't feel close to him or her. What we're telling ourselves at these times we need to learn not to take so seriously — unless there's abuse involved — for it is mostly just the voice of hurt or self-importance in reactive headgear.

Our challenge, our ongoing labor of love, is to be as intimate as possible with whatever is occurring, including our and our partner's stuckness, reactivity, or closed-off-ness. It is, of course, easier (especially at a me-centered stage) to spot the other's stuckness and hold it accountable for ours. Why this is not funnier simply highlights the sticky-ness of our stuckness.

It's not so easy to be intimate with the difficult stuff within when we're in it up to our eyeballs. But after a certain point — the length of which provides an accurate measure of our self-inflicted suffering — what else is there to do? How much longer do we really want to grind away at our consistently unsatisfying righteous waltz of avoidance? How much more can we milk it for it's-not-fair handouts?

Being intimate with the difficult stuff is not about feel-good payoffs, but rather about not losing touch with what-really-matters, however fragile or slippery our connection to that may seem to be. Spending some time openly feeling — feeling *into*, feeling *through*, feeling *for* — our closed-off-ness to our partner opens us, if only by widening the cracks in whatever self-possessed containers we are busy occupying. Not so easy this is, given that we — particularly if we're in a me-centered stage *or* state — may not be feeling very much like taking a break from our funk or nasty mood or whatever else is so seemingly important that we've allowed it to literally possess us.

But when we are deep in the muck — caught up in feeling doubtful or otherwise negative about our relationship with our beloved other — we can at least acknowledge that that is where we are, however embarrassing it might be to us. This is where we can very profitably drop all blame and stop indulging in reactivity (which may sometimes *appear* to be far from reactive!), and also in any self-condemnation for being reactive. (Reactivity will be the topic of Chapter 8.)

And we might as well also drop any romantic notions we have regarding being-centered relationship and mature monogamy — difficulties will, to whatever degree, continue to happen, reactivity will not disappear, and obstacles large and small will continue to cross our path — regardless of what stage of relationship we're occupying — and thank God for this, for without it and the discomfort it provides, we would very likely stay stuck, too cozily snuggled into our daily life's automaticities to awaken from the entrapping dreams we habitually occupy.

This use of discomfort — this willingness to allow our suffering to be a form of grace — generates gratitude in the revelatory raw (especially as we enter being-centered relationship), gratitude for what we "normally" do not feel any gratitude, gratitude for simply being alive, and gratitude for having the capacity to make wise use of difficult conditions.

And what gets us back on track? Sometimes making and taking enough time to let what has happened settle; sometimes letting another's pain really touch us; sometimes remembering what-really-matters. Mostly, though, it simply is a matter of becoming more fully present. Even if we are in a seriously endarkened state, we can be present in it and *to* it, and we can also *remember* to love, regardless of how stony or numb or reactive we may feel (this is most difficult at the me-centered stage of relationship, but nevertheless can still be applied there).

This does not mean that our heart will necessarily open very easily, but it does mean that a seed of awakening is being nourished. What else can we do when we are off track, and recognize that this is so, other than locate, nourish, and fuel our intention to get back on track? As we lift our heads from the mud, we are akin to the first creatures that left the sea and found themselves on land, wriggling free enough of their past to take in the sky.

So many clouds, shapeshifting in multiple speeds, coming and going, long-lasting and short-lived, silver and black and creamy and drenched in fiery splendor, cloud after cloud, all passing through an achingly immense purity of sky. We fundamentally *are* that sky, home to every one of our qualities, containing both thunderbolt and ethereal wisp, already having room for all, already beyond whatever we take ourselves to be, yet always right here, exactly here, remembering when we are clouded by difficulties that whatever is happening is only part of what is *really* happening.

This we cannot truly figure out or explain, but only embrace, letting it remind us of who and what we are. Thus do we expand our love. Thus do we touch what has always touched us. Thus do we go on, gradually lessening our demand that our path be straight, until we are not only walking Freedom's pathless path, but in a very real sense *are* that path. This is not the end, but the *beginning* of a truly human life — and what a joy, what grace, what a miracle of mutuality, what a sacred privilege, to do and share this with another!

Chapter Seven

MATURE MONOGAMY: SOME FURTHER THOUGHTS

Mature monogamy is not only a way of being and a practice, but also an art, existing not so much *outside* the confines of conventional culture, as *beyond* it.

Put another way, mature monogamy primarily arises not on the *horizontal* outskirts of the conventional (where nonconformity flourishes, dressing up in various nonconventional habits and practices), but rather as part of a *vertical* dimension of relationality that cannot be known until we start rubbing the sleep out of our I's, outgrowing both conformity and nonconformity.

That is, mature monogamy is not a different *state* of relationship, but rather a different *stage* of relationship.

In mature monogamy, whatever arises is not so much related *from*, as it is related *to*, through a radically intimate (and therefore deeply but discerningly inclusive) mutuality.

This means, among other things, that the qualities which characterize immature monogamy are neither trashed nor treated as though they don't exist — for many of them likely still will arise — but rather are kept in healthy perspective. They get to come along for the ride, but don't get to do the driving.

Mature monogamy is not something that we can adopt just because it sounds like a good idea; we have to be *ready* for it. And how do we get ready? By exposing, exploring, and ceasing to be a pawn of our conditioning; by turning *toward* our pain; by doing practices that help wake us up; by putting our passion into leaving our prisons rather than into trying to make them cozier, sexier, or more secure. Doing such deep work on ourselves does not necessarily always lead to mature monogamy, but makes it truly possible.

Those of us residing — or *doing time* — in monogamous relationships that, more often than not, are growth-stunting and passion-dulling will not have a real chance at mature monogamy until our longing to be *truly* free is permitted to become stronger (or more consistently central) than our desire to continue distracting ourselves from our suffering.

We may try many strategies to make ourselves feel better — erotic, narcotic, despotic, quixotic, and so on — but what we really need to do is *together* face what is life-draining and growth-stunting and passion-dulling in our relationship, and then do whatever is necessary to get to the root of it.

This may mean, among other things, being willing to face the possibility that we and our partner might have to separate — doing deep work does *not* necessarily guarantee that we will stay together. Perhaps our bond can evolve into one of mature monogamy, and perhaps not. But if we do the necessary work, we will become capable of mature monogamy, whether with each other or another. And even if we don't go into further relationship, the work we will have done will benefit us immensely in whatever we do.

In immature monogamy, we are basically just having an affair with our partner's *potential*, as well as with their conditioning.

But in mature monogamy, we are in relationship with our partner's here-and-now being; we are not seduced by their potential, and nor are we locked into their conditioning. Instead, we know our partner's conditioning almost as intimately as our own, and are able to keep it in ego-transcending perspective, letting ourselves be *awakened*, rather than constrained or diminished, by it.

Rather than exploiting the possibilities of our bond (which only turns our bond into a bind) so as to make ourselves feel better or more secure, we instead heal, awaken, and come fully alive *through* our wholehearted, passionately committed participation in it. Mature monogamy is both crucible and sanctuary — in it, love, awareness, passion, and integrity function as one, generating an intimacy that truly *transforms.*

Long the wait has been
Long the time between
Hold my all in yours
As I hold yours in mine
Can't count all the doors
Can't remember all the dying
But I do remember you
I love this timeless rendezvous
And love that you love it too

Through the holy deep we go
In this love-sealed container for two
Stretching beyond our every disguise
Permitting ourselves our true size
Without cracking the vessel
Connected to the core
Not needing anything more

Energy's awake and on the loose
Flowering bright and everwild
Without us doing a thing
Blossoms of the Real
Bouquets of infinite artistry
And upon our shared palm
Rest a few dying petals
Looking a lot like you and me
So purely and surely themselves
Revealing everything necessary
In their tiny and blazingly brief
And immensely vivid moment
Giving us enough time
To do what we must

In the long darkness you come to me
Your flesh overflowing with light
I take off my face so I can see
And am rewarded by the night
Now the sky's ablaze with dawn
The clouds outlined by my blood
Emptied of me am I, but not gone
Swept away by your ecstatic song
Take me, love, take me to us
Through all our dreams' debris
Let's travel the other side of all the fuss
Where love only deepens the mystery

I've fallen hard once again
You catch me in your glance
And out spills all my pain
Until once again I can dance

I awaken entwined with you
Your all and mine such a fine fit
Freed are we through and through
Knowing we've come too far to quit
In the time beyond time you come to me
Reminding me of our long shared ground
And so I pour into our everfresh familiarity
Feeling a love unbound inside and all around

I've fallen hard once again
You cup my fall with your love
And out spills all my pain
And the joy, the joy that overflows
The joy, the joy that speechlessly knows

II. Working with the Difficult Stuff

Chapter Eight

REACTIVITY

To react means to act again and to do so without awareness, *automatically* reanimating a particular behavioral pattern.

Reactivity is impulsive, even reflexive, regardless of the sophistication or cleverness of its content or delivery. It is self-justifying, predictable, and usually no more than just a waste of time and energy. It is simply us mechanically submitting to our conditioning, while simultaneously acting as if we are not doing so — and usually getting even more reactive if our partner dares to point out to us that we are being reactive.

The key to working with reactivity is to wake up in the midst of it, ideally as close to its inception as possible. Getting familiar with the various signs that signal the arising and presence of reactivity in us is essential, as is making sure that our partner knows these signs (chances being that they already know them better than we do!) and has our full permission to point out their presence to us when we are being reactive, or are about to become reactive.

If you find it especially difficult to wake up from (or snap out of) your reactive trance, allow your partner to help you do so. He or she might, for example, tell you that you're showing the signs of reactivity (as previously explored, clarified, and agreed upon by both of you), or might make a sign, like holding up a hand (again, as previously agreed upon by both of you), or say something that serves as a reminder, like "remember" or "stop" (once again, as previously agreed upon by both of you).

It's essential here that your partner behave with integrity; if they do one of the practices suggested above with *any* intention of overpowering, undermining, morally standing above, or otherwise diminishing you and whatever agreement you had both made regarding such reactivity-interrupting practices, your relationship will be on shakier ground, its stability infected by mistrust.

It is crucial that you *choose* to trust your partner when they bring such practices to your attention while you're in the throes of reactivity, unless there are clear signs that trust is not warranted — do not question their integrity unless you are sure that they are slipping, and do not take what they are saying as just another excuse to remain reactive. Even with a clearly open, consistently high-integrity partner, we may still, in our reactive trance, view them as untrustworthy (perhaps because mistrust has long been part of our default when we have been in any sort of confrontation).

Dealing with reactivity, whether it is ours or our partner's, can be quite a slippery undertaking, heavily infused with regression, righteousness, projection, exaggerated self-protection, and chronic mistrust. Reactivity is also a territory devoid of love; this is an extremely useful thing to know, a no-brainer when we are settled into our basic sanity, but easy to forget when we're busy being reactive. Simply noticing and openly acknowledging during our reactive times that we are *not* being loving, or are *not* feeling love, or are close-hearted, can be enormously helpful. If we can tell our partner that our heart is closed to them, and say this without making them responsible for it, we're then already well on our way out of our reactivity.

Me-centered couples are, given their egocentric orientation, reactive much of the time, whether actively or passively. Practices which help expose and cut through reactivity at best usually only get lip service. The quality of awareness needed to recognize reactivity for what it is barely exists; most of the couple's attention gets siphoned into the rituals through which they maintain their identity.

We-centered couples are less reactive, and ordinarily do not let their reactivity build up a full head of steam. They typically defuse reactivity not by seeing through it and harnessing its energies for more life-giving purposes (as do being-centered couples), but by either getting more superficial with each other (if they are codependent) or emotionally withdrawing from each other (if they are coindependent), choosing behaviors that contrast with their reactive behavior, however artificial that might seem to be.

So if they are thinking negatively, a key strategy might be to think positively, rather than to examine the actual process of thinking itself. Another key strategy might be to disengage from further contact. Such time-outs can be helpful at times, but when they are overused they simply deaden the relationship.

We-centered couples basically deal with reactivity by taking the passion out of it (if they are codependent), or by getting so far away from each other that reactivity has much less impact (if they are coindependent). But whether we turn down the heat or remove ourselves from it, we are still avoiding it.

And being-centered couples? They are rarely reactive, and then only for very short bursts. They treat reactivity as simply sloppy engagement, in need not of suppression, flattening, or avoidance, but rather of the light and care of awakened attention. The energy of reactivity is usually not shut down, but instead is stripped of its *viewpoint*. The way reactivity is worked with at this stage is as compassionate as it is efficient, as mindful as it is passionate. Humor is often present, especially as the absurdities of reactivity's certainties are exposed.

There is not any fear of reactivity in being-centered couples, for it is not a threat to their relationship, and they *know* it. The very arising of reactivity is recognized as an opportunity to get even closer, through mutually exploring some challenging relational terrain.

Reactivity is a kind of laziness. We don't have to work very hard at getting reactive, at least compared to getting nonreactive. It's as easy as sliding downhill. Cutting through reactivity is a very different ride, however, the movement being from reactivity *unseen* to reactivity *seen* to reactivity *seen through*.

Once reactivity is seen through (or rendered transparent), it is replaced by *responsiveness*. And to access such transparency, vulnerability is essential, the kind of vulnerability that doesn't keep itself hidden until our partner shows some vulnerability.

It is important not to set too high or lofty a standard when working with reactivity — after all, we can, in our ambition to be nonreactive, easily pollute ourselves with purity! Sometimes it can be helpful to cut our partner *some* slack when they're feeling reactive. Allowing them to openly express their reactivity for a short time — so long as it is *not* abusive — may get them going energetically, breaking up zones of congestion and stuckness.

Once they are underway, *then* we can interrupt their reactive ritual in a firm yet clearly caring way, realizing that even if they understand what they are doing, and clearly appreciate our having stepped in front of their reactivity, they may still need to cut loose, at least for a little while longer, in a seemingly reactive and likely intense and noisy manner, having what could be called a *conscious rant* (for more on this, see Part 4 of Chapter 18).

Become aware of the roots of your reactivity. Notice how and to what degree your current behavior is tied in with your history, including your early years. Don't overlook the value of such exploration. Connect the dots, and not just intellectually. Doing reactivity-reducing practices is helpful, but is more beneficial when coupled with work that clarifies and directly deals with the origins of our behavioral patterns. Connecting current hurt with long-ago hurt — including with regard to how we handled and still handle it — is very useful.

Meet your partner in their reactivity not with any sense of condescension (for example, "Here you go again!" [eyes rolling] or "Why don't you be more of a man?") or spiritual superiority or any other shaming behavior, but instead with a no-bullshit yet caring presence. No putdowns, and no blind compassion either (for more on blind compassion, see Chapter 12). No shaming, no blaming, no pejorative naming. No overpowering, no crumbling, no deadening.

So what about when both partners are simultaneously caught up in reactivity? At such times, the old "he said, she said" back-and-forth can easily escalate into an ugly encounter featuring favorite hits like "never give an inch" and "it's your fault." When the reactivity has passed, go over what happened in detail — without getting retriggered! — and cocreate some agreements on what to do when things get reactive again. Yes, these agreements will likely not be much more than confetti in a hurricane the next few times there's a reactive bout, but if both partners are sincere about making a change, at some point one of them will wake up in the midst of a mutually reactive bout and stop participating in it, which will, in most cases, serve as a braking force for the other's reactivity.

If possible, they should get themselves into couples therapy without delay, hopefully with a therapist who works not just cognitively, but also directly with body, emotion, and spirituality. Understanding becomes much more potent when it is physically and emotionally congruent, and such a coming together of mind, body, and feeling becomes even more useful when it is brought into fruitful proximity with the kind of perspective that's possible through spiritual practices like meditation (which do not necessarily have to lose any of their power when secularly framed for those who might be uncomfortable with things religious or spiritual).

Be it flat or passionate, soft or hard, frowning or smiling, hostile or passive-aggressive, loud or muted, intellectually or emotionally centered, reactivity remains no more than a mechanical, close-hearted phenomena. It is unillumined egoity's way of conducting business. And it is *potentially* also a way beyond the programs and machinations of egoity, through the very exposure it gives them — when we wake up in the midst of our reactivity, there is no mistaking what needs be worked with!

As we move toward being-centered relationship, reactivity becomes less of a drag, and more of a *catalyst* for deepening our capacity to stay present during difficult times. When we can be nonreactive during our reactivity — that is, *having a bad day well* — without any dissociation from what's going on, we are on track for the greatest ride of all.

Chapter Nine

CONFLICT

The good news about conflict in an intimate relationship is that more often than not it brings out the worst in us (other circumstances can, of course, also do so, but they generally lack the unusually close, no-exit quarters *and* safety that intimate relationship can provide), exposing it to such a degree that it can be worked with in ways that benefit all involved. The bad news is that most couples don't use conflict this way, either indulging in its dramatics or bypassing it, thereby leaving it unresolved (except perhaps superficially).

For me-centered couples, conflict mostly just erodes the relationship. Integrity usually goes out the proverbial window when conflict arises, along with respect for each other. Anger not only heats up, but loses its heart and vulnerability, mutating into aggression and its attack-other operational hardness.

And, at the same time, the taking of responsibility easily slides into the righteous dishing out of blame, as accusatory forefingers, stiff with indignation, busy themselves flailing and fencing, generating through their stabbing certainties a no-one's-land where being right is generally made much more important than being happy or actually caring about our partner.

Conflict in me-centered relationship is not much more than reactivity on a righteous rampage — a tempest in a me-knot. And conflict resolution? It usually means that one partner resolves to give in to the other. One ego gets on top, the other goes under, and the relation-ship does its time upon stagnant waters, buoyed up not only by pleasurable distraction, but also by the fact that so many others are in the same boat — if they are all doing it, then maybe we're on the right track, doing the best we can, etcetera, or so our thinking might go. (The folly of this type of logic is perhaps best seen through taking it to an extreme, as illustrated by the following declaration: Eat shit — ten billion flies can't be wrong.)

We-centered codependent couples do a bit better, having a deeper understanding of conflict. Unfortunately, their understanding does not usually translate into working through conflict in more than merely superficial ways. Conflict is seen as a threat to the relationship, with the result that its energies are not allowed their full aliveness, but are instead diluted, suppressed, or shipped to the outskirts of the relationship.

In we-centered coindependent couples, things are much the same. The understanding of conflict is more sophisticated, but there often is an unhealthy detachment from it, a mutual removal, so that the intersubjective (or "we") space of the relationship remains relatively skirmish-free, but anaemic. Conflict is still viewed as a threat, but not so substantially. And, even if conflict *is* viewed as an opportunity for growth, this remains mostly just an intellectual notion.

And being-centred couples? They don't mind conflict (and don't take conflict to mind, at least for very long), and even welcome it, for they know, right to their core, that its presence is a harbinger of further growth and intimacy. Conflict — which occurs far less often than in earlier stages — gives them not only the opportunity to test, use, and further refine their relational skills, but also the sobering satisfaction and, yes, even exhiliration, of staying present and open-eyed in the midst of stormy and otherwise challenging situations.

Theirs is the art of being together no matter what the weather. Though they may momentarily make a fuss about being right, it usually doesn't take very long to get to the heart of the matter. They also recognize and make good use of the fact that each time they work through a conflict, they are brought closer, their relationship having been honed just a little more deeply.

Conflict brings out our longtime strategies for dealing with stress. Ways of taking care of ourselves when we were young — ways that once helped us survive — very often surface during times of conflict, and are, regardless of how dysfunctional they may be now, frequently still employed as if they will actually help.

If, for example, dissociating or shutting down was our default as a child when things got difficult (perhaps giving us a needed inner remove from an abusive parent), then in times of conflict we are probably still going to resort to it as an adult, while rationalizing its usage.

Conflict gives our neuroses center stage, where we, often with little or no awareness, act them out, perhaps allowing them to refer to themselves as *us*. But as we start to wake up to what we are actually doing, we begin to suspect the presence of a script or program somewhere, if only behind our forehead, that up to now we have let reduce us to puppets.

Intimate relationship can, to varying degrees, be a healing container for this mutually scripted — and mutually enmeshed — arena of suffering and suffering-reinforcing solutions, providing not only mirrors for it, but also enough caring and safety to reach and pass through the pain at the heart of the conflict.

Adopting a nonproblematic orientation to conflict doesn't necessarily mean that conflict will go away, but that it will serve rather than erode our relationship. And how do we do this?

For starters, acknowledge it. Name it.

Deepen your perspective. If there's reactivity going on, you won't be able to do much about it if you insist on continuing to look through its eyes and speak from its perspective. Step back not from the energetics of what is going, but rather from the *drama* of it. There are many ways of deepening *your* perspective — like meditative practice — and all that's needed is that you start practising whichever ones work for you, and continue practising.

Listen. *Really* listen.

Get intimate with your anger.

Get to know it so well that you can express it, however intensely, without getting righteous or aggressive or blaming. Without easy access to your anger — your *clean* anger — you will not have properly functioning boundaries, for anger is, among other things, the key guardian of our boundaries.

You don't have to stop fighting, but rather have to learn how not to let your fighting get the best of you. Yes, anger can demolish relational intimacy, but it can also serve, protect, and deepen it. It all depends on how we use our anger.

Practice receiving your partner's anger — assuming of course that it is not abusive or overdone — and keep practising until you can let it in without shrinking, disappearing, retaliating, or putting up a wall. (This will be explored in plenty of detail in Chapter 18, which is all about anger.)

Be vulnerable — not beaten-down vulnerable, but firmly anchored, standing-tall, non-contracted vulnerable.

Deepen your capacity for empathy and compassion. And do *not* limit compassion to a soft or gentle delivery; there are times when a more fiery expression of compassion may be what is needed.

Get intimate with your fear.

In entering our fear, we end our fear of it. Through attending closely, caringly, and carefully to the particulars of our fear, we *decentralize* it, so that its intentions and viewpoint can no longer govern us.

When we meet our fear with real caring, it de-tenses and de-compresses, usually quite quickly becoming something other than fear, something unburdened by fear's agendas or headlines. Fear met with an open heart does not usually take long to dissolve (see Chapter 19).

If confrontation remains too scary for you, go to a good psychotherapist and explore the roots of your fear of confrontation. The chances are that you learned early that confrontation meant danger or the loss of love or something of similar import. Facing this, and seeing how it has played out in your life, and then working through your fear of confrontation (this being much more than just a cognitive undertaking!) is a profoundly healing and empowering journey.

Such are some of the ingredients of a nonproblematic orientation toward conflict. The mixing bowl — your intimate relationship — is supplied. All you need add is your attention and energy.

In the presence of awakened intimacy, conflict is just shit auditioning to be compost. The me-centered don't see the shovel; the we-centered codependent see it but don't pick it up; the we-centered coindependent pick it up but don't use it, except to scratch the surface; and the being-centered use it, digging deeply and vigorously.

Thus do we prepare the ground for further growth.

Chapter Ten

SHADOW-WORK

Shadow elements are those qualities and traits of ours that typically are kept in the dark — at least from *our* own unobstructed view — and projected onto others, both on personal and collective levels. This creates the frequently very convincing illusion that such elements (*our shadow*) don't belong to us. Exposing and cutting through this until there no longer is any disowning of — nor any investment in disowning — our shadow (and whatever constitutes it) is the essence of shadow-work.

So how does this work in intimate relationship? The first step is to wake up enough to see what is actually going on, and then to name it. For example, we are angry at our partner for speaking unkindly to us earlier in the day, and are busy flaying her or him with righteously logical invective for being so unkind, letting our anger mutate into aggression. We're raising our fist and pointing our forefinger, not seeing that three of our fingers are pointing back at us, especially at our own unkindness. As soon as we allow ourselves to see this, there's a mini-interruption of our neurotic ritual; and if we take it a step further, and name what we are doing — being reactive, hostile, aggressive, and so on, all projected onto our partner — we further our braking and widen our view.

The next step is to communicate what's going on, confessing our inner whereabouts, and to do so *non-defensively*. Vulnerability and transparency are needed here, but even if they are not particularly present, we can still communicate *that*. Such self-generated whistleblowing may be quite difficult to put into action, however, if we're carrying much shame regarding our not doing things better. We may in fact so very quickly convert our shame (regarding, for example, our having projected our own shortcomings or darker elements onto our partner) into other emotions or states — like anger (directed at our partner or at ourselves), shutting down, or dissociation — that we render ourselves almost incapable of speaking up with any clarity or conviction.

But we can still communicate even *that*, if only through a pre-agreed-upon signal of some sort (like touching our mouth with our forefinger). The point is not to provide ourselves with an out — instead of our partner backing us into a corner or confronting us, we do it ourselves. Yes, this is often tough — and will likely bruise our egoity — but it is doable, and necessary if our relationship is to truly mature.

In me-centered relationships, shadow-work isn't usually taken very far, because there is too much investment in being right, and too little in awakening to what is actually occurring. Projection runs rampant, much like it did between the United States and Russia during the Cold War. The me-centered couple has so much unexamined shadow material going on in — and *running* — each member that their relationship is not much more than a no-one's-land wherein both skirmish for control, or one runs roughshod over the other, flag held high. A truly hollow victory.

Things are less extreme in we-centered relationships. The battlefield becomes more an arena of diplomacy and negotiation. Some shadow elements are identified, but are not worked with very deeply. A mild (and sometimes not-so-mild) suppression of our undesirable elements tends to take precedence over expression and breakthrough. We may, for example, dream of a large scary animal that is pursuing us, and might later recognize that it is the embodiment of something we are scared of (or are avoiding) in ourselves — like our power or raw animality — but we're not likely to dive very deeply into exploring this, settling instead for a merely intellectual understanding, with little or no protest from our partner. Our relationship may be afloat upon a stagnant sea, but at least it's afloat. A truly shallow victory.

In being-centered relationships, adversarial and diplomatic stances toward the shadow of both partners are replaced by a mutually compassionate, side-by-side facing of whatever is disowned, marginalized, rejected, or neurotic in *both* partners. Now a real intimacy can be developed with the shadow elements of each.

Here we not only face what has been disowned in us, but also get close enough to it — letting ourselves feel it so fully and deeply that in a sense we *are* it — to free up its energies without, however, taking on its viewpoint, until it is no longer an it, but only *reclaimed us*. This is true integration, organic and real and felt right to the core.

The more deeply we dive, the less we mind upsetting waves, discovering in intimate relationship an increasingly compelling invitation to find freedom *through* our shared heart, our shared history, our shared body, our shared limitations, our shared mortality, our shared being, and, yes, our shared shadow.

Me-centered relationships tend to disown shadow material; we-centered tend to only intellectually own it; and being-centered fully own it.

Me-centered relationships are mostly shadow-driven, we-centered mostly shadow-avoiding, and being-centered shadow-integrating.

What really matters is not so much the presence of our shadow-side, as the kind of relationship we choose to have with it.

May we neither be blinded by light nor keep our shadow in the dark, but instead become truly intimate with it, tossing it neither meat nor religion, bringing to it a compassion that is both clear-hearted and disarmingly powerful, a compassion simultaneously fierce and tender. Such deep care helps transform our shadow, so that its energies serve, rather than obstruct, our well-being.

Chapter Eleven

EMOTIONAL ILLITERACY

We're born feeling. We live feeling, and we die feeling. Even when we might assess ourselves as feeling nothing, there nevertheless is some kind of feeling — including the feeling of numbness — going on, however much it might be in the background. An emotion, and another emotion, and another, layer upon layer, suffusing our flesh, minds, psyches.

But how well do we know our emotions? How much at home are we with them? Do we have difficulty controlling or expressing certain emotions? When fear, anger, shame, or sadness arise, what do we do? We may know our IQ, but do we know our EQ (emotional intelligence)?

Emotional illiteracy — or a lack of emotional sensitivity, understanding, and savvy — is largely rooted in the historical (and still commonplace) devaluing of emotion relative to cognition. Many of us still tend to view emotions as being lower or more primitive than reason, doing little more than clouding the skies of rational thought or muddying objectivity.

Thinking clearly is thus often associated with dispassion, or a muting of our emotions; moral decisions are allegedly best made when passion and feeling are either "safely" out of the picture, or kept functionally peripheral to the decision-making process, much like children excluded or kept at a distance from parental discussions.

Implicit in this attitude is the all-too-common identification of emotion with subjectivity — at least in the sense that subjectivity is a *failure* to be objective — an identification that may be justifiable if and when emotion *is* irrational or ego-centered, but not when it is rationally informed.

We can be objective *and* emotional at the same time, as when a releasing of tears washes away an ossified or neurotically dug-in stance, leaving us not in a particular position, but rather aware *of* possible positions. As research shows, the openly felt, unrepressed presence of emotion can significantly contribute to mental and social skills.

The practice of distancing or dissociating ourselves from our emotions, including our darker or more uncomfortable emotions, can seriously disrupt our ability to think clearly and act with moral intelligence. Research indicates that an impairment in emotional capacity (as perhaps caused by damage to brain regions essential for emotional processing) can actually retard our ability to make sound decisions. Feelings are needed for making truly rational decisions. Without emotional intelligence (EQ), intellectual intelligence (IQ) means little.

Are ethical decisions best conducted in the absence of emotions? Not necessarily. If emotions are ways of dealing with and evaluating our world, then they are *already* deeply implicated in ethics, whether at the level where emotion is little more than a sense of liking or disliking, or at the level where emotion is a complex, somatically rooted yet cognitively sophisticated — and perhaps even rational — "reading" of a given situation.

To view emotions as lower or less reliable than reason also has serious gender implications, given that femaleness is commonly associated with getting emotional, and maleness with being rational. This is roughly paralleled by those views that claim that the neocortex, associated with rational thought, is "higher" than the phylogenetically older zones of the brain that supposedly "house" and deal with emotions — which implies that men, being supposedly more rational, are therefore more developed than women. "You're being emotional!" remains much more of a putdown than "You're being rational!"

Many factors must be taken into account in examining a particular emotion, not the least of which is the interrelatedness of the various emotions. Anger may be a defense against sadness, or sadness may be a defense against anger. Rage at its peak may suddenly metamorphose into joy. Surfacing sadness or anger might trigger shame, and surfacing shame might lead to sadness or anger. Mix together shame and fear, and you'll probably get guilt. When anger and disgust mingle, contempt arises. And so on.

To become emotionally literate, we have to become intimate with our emotions, knowing them from the inside, as well as knowing both our repressive and expressive tendencies regarding them.

As obvious as it may sound, we need to know what we're feeling when we're feeling it. On the way, we must learn to find the balance between *containment* (as when our anger is about to turn into aggression) and *expression* (as when our held-in anger needs to be given emphatic voice). Healthy restraint and healthy uninhibitedness.

We need to learn how to regulate our emotions, how to directly express them, how to infuse such expression with awareness and compassion, how to ride, guide, and ultimately just be with our emotions.

Emotional illiteracy infects most me-centered and many we-centered relationships, regardless of how cleverly it might be covered — or *compensated for* — by "rational" discourse. Despite the obvious presence of emotion in everyone, as well as the equally plain-to-see emotional difficulties many of us have, *emotional education* has yet to take its place in the public school system. It simply does not appear to be a priority for those in charge of educational — or, better, *schooling* — policy. Intellectual intelligence gets the lion's share of attention, with moral and emotional intelligence getting far too little focus.

During couples' work when I ask men what they are feeling, many do something other than say what they are *actually* feeling: They may, for example, state that they "feel" that their partner is not understanding or hearing them, or that they "feel" that they are not getting enough sex or recognition or appreciation (which are statements about what they are *thinking*, not feeling!); or they may look away, and then say something inappropriately abstract, trying to keep the conversation from getting "emotional" or vulnerable; or they may wait in silence for more than a pregnant pause, trying to figure out what to say, until I probe further, at which point they often will state that they are feeling nothing, or that they don't know what they are feeling. And so on. The very question "What are you feeling?" thus becomes an occasion for saying anything but what is *actually* being felt.

By contrast, when I ask women during couples' work what they are feeling, the majority are quick to directly, and usually quite expressively, articulate their emotional state. Of course, what they may actually *do* with their emotional state is another story, but the very fact that they generally recognize what they are feeling and can usually get that across with sufficient accuracy puts them, with few exceptions, far ahead of their partners when it comes to sharing what's occurring emotionally.

Some men, having realized their partner's superior emotional literacy, honor her for it and are inspired by her example to develop the same capacity in themselves. Other men, more me-centered and feeling less positive about their partner's superior emotional literacy, invest much of their energy in finding fault with her delivery, trying to turn the focus back on her, doing what they can to corrall the conversation into a more "civilized" or "reasonable" discussion, *head*-lined by disembodied rationality and the "safety" it provides for his egoity.

It's no accident that the accusation "You're being too emotional" is not paralleled all that often by the accusation "You're being too rational" (although "You're in your head!" is becoming more commonplace). So long as we equate being emotional with being female, and being rational with being male, we are not available for true intimacy. We need to divest emotionality and rationality of any fixed gender associations, and realize, right to our marrow, that emotion and rationality work best when they work *together*.

In intimate relationship it is essential that we, male or female, can clearly state what we are feeling *as we are feeling it*. What we are then conveying is *data*, rather than opinion ("I'm feeling angry" or "I feel sad" are not opinions, but facts, whereas "I feel you're not there for me" or "I feel like you don't see me" are not facts, or even feelings, but opinions). Couples stuck in dead-end arguments and power struggles usually go back and forth with emotionally-charged opinions, sparring over who's right or who's to blame or who's the screwed-up one (or the *more* screwed-up one). What is being felt then is not being simply and directly shared, but instead used to amplify or arm a particular position.

The first step is to identify what you are feeling. If you are feeling sad, simply notice that, without getting caught up in the details or accompaning dramatics. If you are feeling a mix of emotions, and it's not clear what's in the mix, simply notice the mix.

If you are not sure what you are feeling, ask yourself, as simply as possible: Am I feeling sad? Am I feeling angry? Am I feeling happy? Am I feeling unhappy? Am I feeling angry? Am I feeling excited? Am I feeling afraid? Am I feeling uncomfortable? And so on — the odds are that you'll get some kind of instant response to each question, usually in the form of a yes, no, or maybe.

If after this, you still are not sure what you're feeling, look a bit deeper, and notice your general feeling tone, even if it is numbness. If you are convinced that you don't know what you are feeling, start by noticing your most obvious bodily sensations, such as tightness in your shoulders, tension in your belly, or whatever breathing pattern is occurring, and so forth, and note that you are indeed experiencing these.

All you have to do is place your attention on whatever it is that you are feeling; often what this means is withdrawing your attention from your thinking processes. There's nothing to figure out here, no need to ask your mind what you're feeling (as many do when they look away and take a long time to answer the question of what it is that they are feeling).

The second step is to *directly* say what you are feeling. No tangents, no drama, no shoulds. At first, you might feel disconnected from what you are saying, as when announcing in a flat or bland tone that you feel angry, but sooner or later, you'll be able to say what you're feeling in a way that conveys, at least to some degree, the felt experience of such feeling. Your facial muscles, tone, posture, and verbal emphases will make it clear that you are feeling angry as you state that you are indeed angry.

The third step is to make sure that your partner is really hearing what you are saying. This means not only that they are registering the facticity of what you are saying, but are also feeling it (which means, among other things, experiencing it not just from the neck up). Most me-centered (and plenty of we-centered) couples don't take the time to do this, relegating the cultivation of empathy to a very peripheral position in the dynamics of their interchange. However, without some empathetic attunement, the dialogue of a couple quickly degenerates into an energy-draining argument, a deadening withdrawal, or a heart-eroding stalemate.

So say what you are feeling, and if you are on the receiving end, let it in, until you can clearly feel it (whether or not you agree with all of the content or storyline), as if you are in your partner's skin. This may not always feel good, but it keeps us from staying holed up in our egoic strongholds.

The fourth step is to get into the details *without losing touch*. The key here is to make continuing to feel (or experientially resonate with) the other more important than whether you disagree or not with their content. Make your connection with each other *primary*, and the working out of relevant details *secondary*. This is far more efficient than trying to deal with such details when you are not sufficiently connected with each other. This also is when it's very easy to get injuriously reactive. If things get sticky, go back to steps one and two, and stay with them for a while. One minute of sharing what's going on emotionally, without bringing in the corresponding details, prevents overwhelm (or emotional flooding), and can significantly shift the energetics of what's happening.

If you are getting really worked up, resist the temptation to get up on a soapbox or to turn the exchange into a courtroom drama, and instead stay with what you are *feeling* (while acknowledging the difference, if any, between your presenting feeling and your underlying feeling — our show of anger, for example, may be covering our hurt). If this is too intense for you — or for your partner — you might, *with* your partner's permission, *briefly* indulge in a clearly-boundaried but full-blooded rant, or take a break, or stop talking altogether, and go more deeply into your core feeling. It's important, of course, to have prior agreements regarding such options.

Notice which emotion or emotions you are least comfortable with, and start moving *toward* them — however slightly or slowly — even though your aversion to them will be pulling at you to move in the opposite direction. Study them closely, getting intimate with them to the point where their arising is no longer such a concern for you, nor a threat to your relationship, but rather just one more opportunity to deepen both your self-knowledge and your relationship. Your darker emotions are *not* the problem; your aversion to them is.

And notice when an emotion is *secondary* to another emotion.

For example, anger often kicks in when sadness is starting to surface, especially in men. When you are telling your partner what you are feeling, you may begin by stating the obvious — e.g., "I'm angry" — but while doing this, pay attention to how *open* you actually are. If you're tight or closed-off, the odds are high that you're feeling *another* emotion and that you also are reluctant to share it, or even to admit that it's there. You might begin here by stating that you are having a difficult time saying what's going on emotionally, besides being angry. Maybe there's some sadness, some hurt, some shame. If we're not being -centered, we will likely have difficulty being vulnerable and nondefensive in difficult exchanges with our partner, finding it easier to be angry than to directly show our hurt.

For all four of the steps described above, being vulnerable — that is, being transparent and open, even to our lack of openness — is immensely helpful, because it keeps an emotionally honest resonance going between the partners, along with an amplified receptivity that invites more in-depth disclosure and sharing.

About being open: This doesn't mean that we're necessarily happy and open-hearted, but rather that we remain aware of and receptive to what is occurring. An honest sharing of one's fear, devoid of any self-protection, can bring a couple very close. In fact, the more we openly expose and share the emotional states (and their historical roots) that we are most afraid to share, the deeper our connection will be.

Emotional literacy is the core of emotional intelligence — which includes emotional awareness, empathy, expressive competency, interpersonal savvy, and other related feeling-centered or feeling-including qualities which influence our ability to succeed in dealing with the demands and pressures of life. Without sufficiently developed emotional intelligence, we easily tend to overrely on other kinds of intelligence, especially the intellectual.

Just as we can raise our IQ, so too can we raise our EQ (emotional intelligence). And how? Through various practices which address the weaker areas of our emotional life. If we score low in empathy, we are not necessarily sentenced to remain there. A little study of empathy, combined with some empathy-generating practices (visualizing ourselves in another's position, learning to listen wholeheartedly to another, doing meditative practices like *metta* or *tonglen*, etcetera), will deepen our capacity for empathy.

If we have trouble reading the emotional weather of our relationship, practising what was described earlier in this chapter (the four steps to emotional literacy) will help us develop a keener sense of what's going on emotionally. This, by the way, requires no lowering of IQ, no intellectual slumming, no shunning of rationality, no triumphant summations of "He's in his head!" In fact, as our EQ goes up, our IQ may also go up, if only because we're now bringing more of us to whatever's before us.

An increased IQ may not mean an increased MQ (moral intelligence), but an increased EQ may well mean an increased MQ, simply because the more in touch we are with the emotional terrain of our intimate other — including having increased empathy for them — the more likely we are to want to treat them better.

And, as we take this further (establishing ourselves in being-centered relationship), extending our empathy and feeling for others to more and more beings, the more we start to understand, in a very visceral and obvious sense, that what we do to another we do to ourselves.

It takes a certain cognitive ability even to consider getting into someone else's skin or shoes (the capacity for empathy is present within 24 hours after birth, but it is not a *chosen* empathy), as well as to recognize that we are indeed doing so (without such recognition, empathy easily can become a negative force, swamping or overwhelming us with another's emotional state), but empathy nevertheless remains primarily a feeling-based undertaking. (Emotion itself blends feeling, cognition, and various social factors.)

If I get lost in your emotional state, then I am going to be of no more use to you than if I were to remain cut off from your emotional state. So part of the challenge during our relational difficulties is to get close enough to our partner to openly feel *their* state, while separating it from our state — and also while keeping enough space between us for focusing purposes.

Another factor to consider here is boundaries. Robert Frost famously said that good fences make good neighbours; in the same spirit, we could say that good boundaries make good connections, and furthermore, keep the integrity of the relationship alive and well.

Letting go of or dissolving our boundaries so as to include the other is not the same as *expanding* our boundaries to include the other.

In openly sharing and exploring our emotions with our partner (and vice versa) — which means not only talking about and fittingly expressing them, but also being upfront about our operational context for such expression — we create, and in a sense are also created by, a vibrantly alive, cartography-transcending "we-space" that is nonetheless far from inaccessible.

Through such multileveled communion, such passionately participatory interconnection, such transparent mutuality, such deeply shared aliveness, we only deepen and enrich our intimacy. Such is the prevailing condition of mature monogamy.

We exist through relationship, and the more emotionally literate we are, the deeper and happier our relationships — and therefore we — will be.

Chapter Twelve

BLIND COMPASSION

Given how essential compassion is to the well-being and deepening of intimate relationship, we need to consistently practice it, which requires, among other things, that we know it well, being familiar not only with what constitutes it, but also with its *surrogates*, key among which are pity and what will in this chapter be referred to as "blind compassion."

Blind compassion is basically just neurotically tolerant, confrontation-phobic, undiscriminating caring.

Blind compassion is commonly centered by the belief that everyone is doing the best that they can. Not surprisingly, blind compassion cuts everyone — *everyone!* — far too much slack, making an ever-so-gentle fuss about not making a fuss regarding whatever behavioral lapse it is taking pains to so kindly address.

Blind compassion does not just act kind when kindness *is* called for, but also when something quite different is *needed*, such as a forceful no, or an umistakable voicing of displeasure, or an anger-defended setting and maintaining of boundaries. Such activities are not in themselves necessarily devoid of love, but whatever love is there is not limited to just a kindly approach.

Blind compassion keeps love too meek, sentenced to wearing a kind or nice face. This is not the kindness of the Dalai Lama, which is strongly rooted in courage, but rather a kindness rooted in fear, and not just the fear of confrontation, but also the fear of not coming across as a good person. The apparent humility of blind compassion is little more than a kind of subtle, piously flattened arrogance, carrying as it does the well-disguised but nonetheless still exaggerated self-worth of being such a compassionate server of others' well-being.

Almost never does blind compassion show any anger, for it is scared to upset anyone. This is reinforced by its negative conceptualizing of anger — especially in its more fiery expression — as something less than spiritual, something to be equated with ill will, hostility, and aggression, something that should *not* be there if we are being truly loving.

Blind compassion has the deluded notion that compassion has to be gentle. Thus does it impale itself on its niceness implants. Blind compassion has no voice other than that of making nice and making excuses. Its articulation is unrelentingly soft and pleasant, brightly buttoned-up. No guts. Being a harmony junkie, blind compassion will do just about anything to keep the peace, so long as it doesn't have to show its teeth in anything other than I-wouldn't-harm-a-fly smiles.

And how very sweetly blind compassion smiles, trying to convey its understanding and caring through an aggressively gentle sympathy. Blind compassion doesn't know how to — or won't — say *no* with any real power, so that its yes is weak, flabby, and enabling of whatever offense it is facing. Practitioners of blind compassion oppose violence, yet violate the very forcefulness they may need to take necessary stands.

Blind compassion confuses anger with aggression, forcefulness with violence, judgment with condemnation, exaggerated tolerance with caring, and spiritual correctness with moral maturity.

Its voice has no belly, no taking-a-stand resonance, no real authority. Its openness is but a permissive hole, a spineless embrace, a weakly enforced dropzone, thickly lined with an undiscerning and foolish sympathy. It may not look afraid, but it is, not only of rocking the boat, but also of losing or straying from its rigidly gentle "doing-good" self-image.

Confusing the Absolute and the Relative is often characteristic of blind compassion. It typically *reduces* the ultimate truth of our real nature to a mere concept, and then *undiscerningly* applies this to the neurotic or abusive behavior of others, spiritually whitewashing or otherwise downplaying such behavior, while eviscerating its own response to it. (An example: "You should not be angry at your rapist, because he is really just part of you and you are just part of him, since we're all one.") As it thus morally deludes — and disempowers — itself, blind compassion keeps on smiling, for in its rendering itself incapable of confrontation, it finds a craved safety or refuge from the more brutal dimensions of life.

Blind compassion is so afraid of (and so *non-intimate* with) our darker aspects that it keeps painting them over with our best qualities. Thus does it keep darkness in the shadows. Recognizing that we each contain all qualities does not mean that we therefore are not responsible for what we *do* with them. Blind compassion doesn't really see this, letting its fixation on the essential goodness — along with its overfocus on the *potential* — of everyone blind it to what's not so good, at least to the degree that it does not take sufficiently strong stands regarding abusive behavior, while acting as if its doing so is somehow virtuous.

Much of this has to do with the popularized notion that we shouldn't judge others. There are some very serious problems with this: First of all, we *do* judge others; judgment is simply one of the things that the mind does, and to make it wrong — that is, to judge our judging — only erodes us and drags us into guilt's stalemated domain, splitting us into "good" (read: *not judging*) and "bad" (read: *judging*) factions. The mind — your mind, my mind, *everyone's* mind — will keep churning out judgments, because that's part of its nature. What really matters is how we handle our judgments: Do we identify with them? Do we take them seriously, and if so, when? Do we allow them to recruit emotional energy? Do we try to rise above them, or pretend that they aren't there?

In short, judging others is not the real issue; what is truly important is how we deal with our judgments. Since they are already there, why not make wise or life-giving use out of them, instead of trying to get rid of them?

The second problem with the notion that we shouldn't judge others is the fact that judgment per se is not necessarily always a negative or useless phenomenon. Strip away the hostile, condescending, or mean-spirited elements that often characterize judgment, and you may find amidst what is left a kernel of valuable insight, or perhaps a timely intuition. Judgment is not necessarily equivalent to condemnation!

If we see others behaving abusively or know for sure that they have thus behaved, and judgment then arises in us, don't make that wrong, for it is but a natural part of our moral response to what they have done. If we look closely, we will see that we are not so much judging them as we are judging their *behavior* — but in any case, we are judging.

This is a major no-no for blind compassion's practitioners, even as they scramble to distance or dissociate themselves from their own judging. If someone has just assaulted your child, are you going to make a problem out of the fact that you are judging that person, and that you are outraged? Are you going to bypass your feelings for what has happened by framing the whole thing in a "higher" light before you've even dealt with the raw reality of it? Probably not, unless you are committed to blind compassion.

When those who espouse blind compassion encounter or hear about offensive behavior from others, they usually take pains not only to be nonjudgmental — or at least not to say or do anything that could be construed as judgmental — but also to examine whatever such behavior may be triggering in themselves, while bringing no real heat to those who actually have been, or are, behaving offensively.

That is, if what you are doing is upsetting me, my job (as a graduate of Blind Compassion 101) is not to focus to any significant degree on *your* behavior, but rather to find out what my being bothered says about *me*, while perhaps also acknowledging and appreciating the opportunity you are giving me to thus examine myself.

This is not only a misguided reading of the art of allowing all things to serve our awakening, but also a far-from-compassionate response to our offending others, for we, in not being on the side of doing what we can to bring them face to face with the consequences of their actions, are on the side of *depriving* them of something they may sorely need. And in letting them off the hook, we are doing the same for ourselves.

Some who practise blind compassion do so for supposedly spiritual reasons (often being drawn to anger-phobic spiritual paths), confusing being loving with everyone with putting up with whatever they do and never, *never* judging them, no matter what they do. Blind compassion's devotees take whatever their teachers do and frame it in a manner that doesn't challenge or confront them. Even clearly abusive behavior on the part of the teacher is excused as a teaching or an opportunity for students to see more of themselves. The old mirror trick...

Others who are caught up in blind compassion may do so for reasons of survival, having learned as children that the best way to deal with confrontational or violent situations was to make nice and to make excuses for the abusive behavior of others (perhaps having learned this by example from a parent who was passively receiving abuse from their spouse). Such people will often say of their parents that they were doing the best they could (even when this included rape and violent beatings), frequently citing their parents' abusive upbringing. Believing this allows us to leave our abusive parents unchallenged; we may say that we don't want to hurt them, that we see no point in bringing up the past with them, that what they did was just a product of their past, and so on, excuse upon excuse.

To cut through this, we would at some point have to directly and openly feel not only the pain of the abuse we suffered, but also its later consequences in our life, and not many of us want to do that, even when we understand the value of doing so, as in therapeutic contexts. We learned back then that saying a clear *no* to the abuse that we were suffering made things even worse, and often continue as adults to avoid saying such a no, fearing, however unconsciously, that doing so is very dangerous (because it truly *was* very dangerous). Practicing blind compassion keeps us "safely" removed both from having to say a strong and unequivocal no, and from the consequences of so doing. This all demonstates how fear-driven blind compassion is.

The belief that everyone is doing the best they can lets everyone off the hook, including us — for then, we don't have to ruffle any feathers, raise any hackles, kick up a storm, make a fuss, or otherwise confront anybody. Such a belief robs us of autonomy and accountability, implying as it does that we don't really have a choice as to what we do. If we view our parents as puppets of their conditioning, then how can we hold them responsible for what they did? After all, they couldn't help it — or could they? There's also a fear of recognizing that our parents *did* make a choice when they abused us, for if we do see this, then what are we going to do? Can we then remain passive children in adult bodies?

When you are being unkind to your partner, and know you are doing so, are you *really* doing your best? And what about when "doing our best" is simply not good enough? For example, if doing my best means that I'm remaining a drug addict and won't get any treatment, then what? Blind compassion frames us as *victims*, and enables us to stay that way, even as it spouts spiritual platitudes about our true nature and our inherent goodness. Blind compassion disempowers us while giving power to the offending other, whereas real compassion empowers us to take the necessary action, however painful that might be, or might have to be.

Blind compassion means well. Unfortunately, its efforts to do good only backfire. It's in such a hurry to forgive that it doesn't make room for the unfolding of what necessarily *precedes* forgiveness; it confuses forgiveness and condoning, trying to pardon the other *before* the behavior in question has been looked at in any real depth.

The very permissiveness out of which blind compassion makes such a virtue simply allows abusive behavior to *continue*, with minimal policing. Consider the famous statement: "I may not like what you say, but I will defend to the death your right to say it." This is talking the talk at its most puffed-up — how many supporters of that proclamation, however strongly they might believe in it, would actually let themselves be put to death so that someone (whom they probably don't even know) could say something they didn't like?

Blind compassion takes many forms and can be found in every area of life, helping worsen the very conditions about which it is concerned. And it can get very sophisticated; consider postmodern thought's refusal to place one value above or below another — in the name of supposed "equality" — and how that has led to a neurotic tolerating of (and also an accompanying secretly-sought-for distancing from) what common sense would call atrocious conditions.

We-centered codependent and me-centered couples are usually more prone to blind compassion than are we-centered coindependent couples, but none are immune to its siren call. Only being-centered couples are free from blind compassion.

So how to deal with blind compassion? Get familiar with it. Don't get pulled into its embrace. See it, name it, and don't blame it. Meet it and its underlying fear with genuine compassion, compassion that's willing to be fiery, fierce, and unsmiling, compassion that's loving enough not to give a damn about being nice.

As blind compassion sheds its blinders and opens its eyes to its own pain, its own anger and hurt and frustration and moral outrage, thereby letting in — and letting out! — a love previously not accessible, it finds its spine, and simply becomes real compassion, with an especially keen and caring eye for those who are still under the spell of blind compassion.

Chapter Thirteen

WORKING WITH JEALOUSY

Jealousy is a painfully intense contractile reaction to — and usually also a *dramatization* of — being rejected or replaced, whether this is real or imagined. Jealousy's ache is one of deep-cutting anguish, burning its way into heart and solar plexus, impaling us on its moral outrage.

Even the slightest threat — however groundless — of being rejected or replaced (or bumped to less-than-central status), may be enough to trigger jealousy, especially if we already do not feel particularly secure or stable in our intimate relationship.

Given jealousy's power to erode and undermine — and, at the extreme, destroy — intimacy, it is extremely important to be able to deal with it skillfully, which begins with knowing it from the inside.

Jealousy can take many forms, ranging from a mildly gnawing sense of being insufficiently wanted to raging or even murderous revengefulness. But whatever its form or appearance, it remains a grippingly unpleasant state that can easily *possess* us.

Jealousy is not so much a single emotion as a blending of a number of emotions, with hurt (the *ache*), grief (the *loss*) and anger (the *moral outrage*) atop the list, followed by shame and resentment, all combining to generate an *achingly* compelling sense of being pushed aside, replaced, unwanted, rejected — that is, relegated from our primary status with an esteemed or beloved other to a less-than-primary status.

Jealousy shows up early in life; toddlers who find a younger sibling on the scene may demonstrate jealousy, as when they — with territorial intensity — aggressively push aside, overrun, or pinch their more youthful competition. (Competition for what? Parental attention, for starters.)

What follows concerns not the morbid or pathological extremes of jealousy, but rather the more commonplace kinds of jealousy — both warranted and unwarranted — which arise when there is a perceived threat to our closeness with our intimate other.

Warranted jealousy arises when our partner has betrayed or is betraying us, through, for example, interacting intimately (and not necessarily sexually!) with another without our permission — and such jealousy may still arise even if we *have* given our permission, especially when such permission-giving came not from our core, but rather from our desire to please or control our partner.

And unwarranted jealousy? It arises when we mistakenly assume that our partner has betrayed us.

Jealousy can be exceedingly painful, as anyone who has writhed in its straitjacketed fires knows all too well. Most of us strive not to provide fertile conditions for jealousy, but it nevertheless may still manage to sprout up, with a green not of sun-embracing reach, but of dark and sometimes venomous force.

However, jealousy is *not* some inherently evil or negative or necessarily inappropriate feeling! If we catch our partner cheating on us, our feeling jealous is far from unnatural — we'll feel a mixture of hurt, grief, anger, resentment, and perhaps also shock, all of it intensified when we think of our partner with his or her new lover. And we'll also probably feel like taking various actions, some of which will only make things even worse (like getting violent), and some of which may help bring about a needed healing (like establishing and maintaining clear boundaries).

What matters is what we actually *do* with our jealousy.

Do we get lost in its dramatics? Do we settle for being right? Do we indulge in revengeful fantasies? Or do we try to rise above our jealousy, acting as if we are beyond it, thereby denying ourselves full access to it and its *possible* riches? Or do we condemn it, sentencing it to a padded cell, thereby walling away the very vulnerability of which our jealousy is but a confession, however twisted or dark? Or do we abstract it, talking about it with relentlessly level, disembodied rationality and unnatural calm, even as we now and then wonder why our emotional life tends to be so flat and unexciting?

Do we believe in our jealousy so strongly that we do harm to ourselves or another? Or do we flee it, avoiding any circumstances that resemble the ones that originally catalyzed our jealousy? Or do we deny that it is actually happening, while we slowly die inside, painting good cheer and non-possessive smiles all over our collapse of heart? Or do we make good use of our jealousy, giving its energies enough room to breathe and move through us, while taking appropriate action?

So how to work with our jealousy?

First of all, acknowledge its presence and *name* it. As blatantly obvious as jealousy can be, we may have trouble— likely shame-based — openly admitting that it is indeed present. Being jealous may not fit into our self-image.

Second, don't try to eradicate your jealousy. Instead, explore it and dig deep, mining its depths for what lies at its core (if possible, work on this with a suitably skilled psychotherapist). Get in touch, and stay in touch, with the hurt, anger, and sense of loss that constitute it.

Third, get your jealousy in healthy perspective; that is, allow it to be there, but don't let it run the show (psychotherapy and meditative practice are very useful here, especially when employed in conjunction).

And last but not least, if your partner has catalyzed (or is catalyzing) your jealousy (as by having an emotional affair), do not let him or her off the hook — as we are prone to do when under blind compassion's spell — and do *not* make yourself wrong for being jealous!

Seat your jealousy where you can keep a clear eye (a non-jealous eye!) on it, so that when it starts to act up, you can spot it immediately and take steps (like shifting perspective) to keep it from overwhelming you. This is not easy, but gets easier with practice.

Jealousy is made possible through attachment. So, not surprisingly, some of us — perhaps seeking an end to jealousy — strive for nonattachment in relationships.

Without attachment, there would be no jealousy (and there would also be no compassion!) — but do not allow yourself to make a problem out of attachment, and *be aware/beware* of teachings which view attachment as something to be shed or transcended (with the exception, of course, of our attachment to such views themselves!).

It's very easy to get attached to not being attached. Yes, attachment does have its pathological possibilities — such as addiction — but it itself is not necessarily a sign of neurosis or immaturity. Attachment comes with relational intimacy (and in fact *deepens* as we become truly closer, even as it simultaneously becomes more transparent).

Jealousy often features a compulsive drive to blame our offending — or *apparently* offending — other for what is happening to us in our jealous state, as if to somehow *legitimize* what we're doing with our jealousy. At the same time, though, it is important that we not downplay what is triggering our jealousy, just because we're not handling our jealousy very well.

The central message of jealousy usually is a blend of (1) "You don't love me!" or something similar, implying colossal or terribly unfair rejection, as of a child by its mother; and (2) "If you *really* loved me, you could *not* and would *not* be doing what you're doing!" This, of course, is reinforced by the fact that our partner's jealousy-catalyzing actions may be far from loving regarding us, including to the point of actual betrayal.

Feeling unloved by our partner hurts, but when it is accompanied by their giving to another what we're aching for them to give to us, it *really* hurts. This is the raw anguish of jealousy, the jagged gut-slam and heart-shock of in-your-face rejection.

It is easy to get marooned in the wastelands of rejection, especially if our history has predisposed us to being readily hooked or triggered by any sign of rejection.

But as we mature, we learn to stay open and present in the midst of *real* rejection, ceasing to let our jealousy run us: There may be anger and tears and indignant disbelief, and all the symptoms of jealousy, but there will be no significant withdrawal of self, nor any indulgence in mere blaming; there may be force, but not violence; there is vulnerability, but not mushiness or self-pity; there is real sadness, not reactive sorrow; and there is a clear willingness to go right *through* jealousy's dark realm, rather than just adopting a righteous positioning somewhere within it; and most of all, there is love — or at least the all-out commitment to making room for it — rather than just an uptight, loveless waiting to see if the other, the one who has rejected us, is being loving, or is going to become loving toward us. (This does not mean, however, that we should be openhearted with our partner after they have betrayed us, but rather that we not lose touch with our heart, even in the midst of our anger and hurt.)

If we will only love when we are *already* being loved by the other (as eptomized by me-centered relationships), we are prime candidates for unwarranted jealousy, for we are then chronically on the search for signs that we are not being loved, miserably sniffing around for evidence of abandonment or neglect or betrayal, reducing ourselves to little more than neurotic sleuths, sinking into overamplified suspiciousness, again and again demanding, however indirectly, that our partner consistently demonstrate or prove his or her trustworthiness.

Such demonstration, however, is rarely enough for us, for we, in the gripping dramatics of our unillumined jealousy, won't trust anything except our mistrust and doubt regarding the other. In short, we then *expect* betrayal, and perhaps even in some sense crave it, so as to recreate (usually unconsciously) childhood scenarios of unresolved rejection.

The lesson here, at essence, is to remain truly open to being loving (in the highest sense), even when we are clearly being rejected. The form of such love is *not* meek or passive, nor necessarily all-accepting of rejection. Rather, it is potent, dynamic, and passionately alive, quite capable of fiery yet clean anger, more than willing to call bullshit bullshit (as when the other deliberately does things to catalyze our jealousy, so as to feel more powerful or more in control). Such love does not shrink for long in the face of rejection, and nor does it piously stand aside or slip into the robes of blind compassion. Instead, it radiates forth, generating an environment that simultaneously cradles reactivity and renders it so transparent that it cannot possess us.

When we get overfocused on feeling rejected — to the point of *identifying* with such feeling — we are, in part, just blocking ourselves from fully feeling our woundedness. We are then, in effect, actually rejecting what is most vulnerable in us, doing to it what is being or was done to us (or what we imagine is being or was done to us) by the one "making" us jealous.

Real love does not reject the other, but it may reject — and may *need* to reject — something that the other is *doing.*

Jealousy is the festering abscess of feeling cast aside, the endarkened sensation of betrayal-catalyzed rejection and loss. When untouched by awareness, jealousy — especially in its unwarranted form — is mostly just a mean-spirited temper tantrum, a coupling of twisted anger and exaggerated hurt up on a toxic soapbox, righteously ranting about right and wrong, making too much noise to hear its own true song.

When held and penetrated by compassion, however, jealousy eases its defences, becoming a raw, nonviolent expression of relational hurt and wounding, a heart-opening confession of in-depth attachment that has been amplified by rejection, an honest sharing of deep feeling, leaving us sobered, unmasked, and more loving, more at ease with our attachment toward our partner (and with our demand for integrity from him or her), no longer struggling for either ownership or detachment, no longer held hostage by the possibility of potential rejection, no longer afraid of jealousy, and no longer so bound to being in relationships that, through their unresolved neurotic patterns and lack of real grounding, provide excessively fertile conditions for the arising of jealousy.

When jealousy arrives, treat it neither as an enemy nor as a green light for reactive behavior, but rather as a challenging visitor. Listen to it closely, separating what is neurotic in it from what is *not.* Stay with it, until its dramatics diminish and its vulnerability and hurt are clearly in the open. *Then* address what spawned it, with attention given to both detail and context, until it's clear if it is warranted or unwarranted.

In the presence of our undivided, compassion-infused attention, our jealousy may flail and rage briefly, but will quickly be but hurt, deep hurt. Don't try to fix, rehabilitate, or spiritualize that hurt. Instead, simply *be* with it, holding it as you would an upset child whom you love. Allow it to shake and weep. Let it breathe fully. Hold it close. When it has settled, then whatever actions may be called for can be sanely considered.

Jealousy is a difficult guest. Treat it as such.

Chapter Fourteen

POWER STRUGGLES

As varied as the literature on intimate relationship is, almost all of it includes some focus on the infamous "power struggle," simply because at various points just about every relationship — except for those already at a being-centered stage — grapples with, and frequently succumbs, to power issues.

In relationships where there doesn't appear to be any power struggle, it's often because one partner is — with no overt fuss — allowing the other to run the show. This, of course, speaks not of resolution, but of resignation (and perhaps also of a potential uprising at some point, if the downtrodden partner somehow someday takes a real stand against the dominating other).

Most couples don't fully resolve their power struggles, settling instead for a partial resolution or negotiated truce, taking comfort in the common territory between them that is no longer under dispute. What hasn't been dealt with is then simply kept in a sufficiently peripheral position so as not to threaten or disrupt the relationship. Still, it does exist, and does show up, if only in dreams (which, more often than not, are either not remembered or not shared, or are shared but not explored in any real depth).

So how do we resolve our power struggles with our partner? First of all, we need to see what we're actually struggling over — we can call it "power," but what exactly is that? Autonomy? Non-interference with what we want? Agreement from significant others? Social strength? The taking of a stand? There are many ways of looking at power, but for now let's say that power is the capacity to act effectively, to generate significant change, to impose our will — in cooperation with others or not — on our environment, human and otherwise.

And for *what* do we need this power for which we are struggling? To remain on top? To not go under? To win? To succeed? To be heard, felt, seen, appreciated, loved, known? The list is long, but no matter what it is that we "need" power for, it exists in a *relational* context.

"Power over" is power over another or others, or over something in us from which we feel separate; "power with" is power shared with another or others; and to be "empowered" is to experience power or an increase in power through another or others. What this all means is that power arises in a reciprocal manner, however imbalanced the dynamic and/or result may be — another or others are involved, however indirectly or fleetingly.

In me-centered relationships, power primarily shows up as *power over*. This can take form as one person overpowering the other (in their childish dependency of two, one plays the boss or parent, the other the employee, child, serf, slave, underling, "support" person, and so on); or it can take form as both partners having a substantial amount of power over the other (in their adolescent independency of two, both take turns playing boss, with the playing field divided up between them). But in any case, the needs of the relationship come in a distant second to the needs of one or both partners.

In we-centered codependent relationships, power primarily shows up as *power to*. To what? To take care of the relationship, with the care of its partners primarily a *secondary* concern. This takes form as a kind of power brokering that makes negotiation between the partners the hub of the relationship. The needs of the relationship thus typically take precedence over the needs of both partners.

In we-centered coindependent relationships, power also primarily shows up as *power to*. To what? To take care of the relationship, but with the care of its partners an *equivalent* rather than secondary concern.This takes form as a mutual pact that finds what intimacy it can through shared separateness. The needs of the partners and the needs of the relationship are mostly kept on a level playing field, so that personal autonomy is not threatened or diminished by the relationship (and vice versa).

In being-centered relationships, power primarily shows up as *power with*. Power struggles don't exist here; there's just not enough fuel for them to get started. They have simply been outgrown. Power at this stage is harnessed not only for the good both of the relationship and the couple, but also for all those associated with them, directly and indirectly. Their power and their love function together with synergistic ease. The needs of the partners and the needs of the relationship exist not in opposition, but in naturally cooperative, finely attuned, ever-evolving symbiosis.

Vulnerability is a source of strength in being-centered relationship. So too is softness, tenderness, subtlety, transparency. And such qualities more often than not seamlessly coexist with great passion, vitality, rawness, and openness, generating tremendous power.

Power is an *ally* at this stage, a force that fuels and drives the relationship, without any diminishment of either partner. Both consistently and naturally empower the other, having no fear of being mistreated or tricked by the other. They have the unshakable power of deep mutual trust. Their shared power fuels their love, and their shared love fuels their power.

Chapter Fifteen

RELATIONSHIP-INFECTING DELUSIONS

1. I won't confront you because I don't want to hurt you.

This and related statements — like "I didn't tell you because I didn't want to disturb you" — may sound good on the surface, perhaps even nobly intentioned, but are no more than denial in caring's clothing, whether consciously or unconsciously animated. They are not really intended to spare our partner pain, but rather to keep us as far as possible from *our* own pain, including that of facing — that is, confronting — what we are actually doing.

How ironic it is that our supposed effort — so nicely dressed — not to hurt our partner actually hurts them, sooner or later, *more* than direct disclosure. In our stated intention not to confront them because we don't want to hurt them, we sound — or at least *want* to sound — as if we *are* there for them and are being considerate, but in reality we are not.

Instead of being straightforward in front of our partner — *upfront* — we are elsewhere, desperately trying not to rock the boat, facing not our partner, but something less challenging (like being resolutely nice).

If we are afraid to confront our intimate other — assuming of course that it is not dangerous to do so — then we need to confront that fear, through our own efforts, or in caring conjunction with our partner, or through professional help. Relationships devoid of confrontation are relationships that are flat, relationships that are more about surviving than thriving, addicted to a numbing by niceness, a deadening that rejects the depths and invests far too much in the shallows.

Just as avoiding death deadens us, so too does avoiding confrontation. Confrontation does not have to be hell! It can be life-enhancing challenge, healthy combat, intimacy-deepening fieriness, as vulnerable as it is intense. Bypassing it only deepens and reinforces our suffering.

2. I'm giving you what you want because it helps keep the peace.

This was, understandably, the mantra of all too many women before the 1960s, and still is for many, despite greatly increased opportunities to go in a different direction. The peace gained by giving in to a hostile or aggressive or overly intense partner is not real peace, but rather only an energetic flattening that lets us off the hook with regard to confronting the very conditioning that animates our disempowered "stand."

There are many women who say that they don't enjoy sex with their husbands, but nonetheless still permit it regularly, because it makes things easier or more pleasant — a crabby or mean-spirited husband is not such a drag to be around after he's ejaculated (his partner then being an outhouse for his frustration or edginess). Trading sex for peace, security, cooperation, care, and so on, is little more than prositution.

But "I'm giving you want you want because it helps keep the peace" is not just a strategy employed by many women; it is also a popular "stand" for many men, not so much in sexual arenas, as in emotional ones.

These men have caved in, crumbling before the superior emotional literacy and/or dominance of their partners, finding a certain security, however deadening, in their emasculation. Trading compliance — with testicles often being the currency — for a ceasefire just keeps us small, "safely" removed from the stands we truly need to take.

"I'm giving you what you want because it keeps the peace" really means "I'm giving you what you want because I'm scared to do otherwise."

3. Trading sex for security within a relationship is not prostitution.

This is a subset of (2), in which we conceptualize our deal — that is, our trade — as something more than it is. I'm not saying that prostitution is always a terrible thing; some women, for example, may, through their prostituting themselves to their husbands for financial security, provide the kind of help that someone else — their children or parents, for example — may desperately need.

Still, it is important to call it what it is. Once we have named it, we can, if our circumstances are not desperate, start to address it, perhaps dealing with the very conditioning that first drove us to prostitute ourselves.

4. I can't live without you.

This is *not* the voice of love, however romantically framed it might be! Desperation is not love, anymore than addiction is. "I can't live without you" is the cry of a victim, whether that victim is a beginner or not, a cry that, however unwittingly, is infused with manipulation. As such, it is but blackmail in need's clothing.

When you encounter another saying "I can't live without you," *fierce compassion* — emanating not only care for that person, but also a suitably firm and, if necessary, fiery *no* to his or her behavior — is the primary remedy. Anything less will drain you.

"I can't live without you" is not a proclamation of love, but of a lazy incompleteness — and I say "lazy" because the one stating "I can't live without you" is wanting (and perhaps also expecting) *you* to complete them, to make them feel better or more whole, instead of actually doing the work of accessing happiness or wholeness themselves.

We can only enter into truly intimate relationship when we *already* are fully functioning without having — or needing to have — such a relationship; yes, we'd love to have it, but we'll still keep on living, and living well, without it. No desperation, no neurotic dependency on another, no looking outside ourselves for wholeness — such are some of the ingredients for real intimacy.

It is very important that we go into relationship not to be made complete or whole, but rather to share, expand, and deepen our *already-established* sense of completeness or wholeness. Then we don't burden relationship with the obligation to make us feel better or more whole, but instead allow it to be an expression and furthering of our love for each other.

5. Making nice makes things better.

"Making nice" simply keeps what is not working in our relationship from any telling intervention. Don't be nice; be real. Being real can mean being soft and gentle, and it can also mean being firm and fiery. Making nice doesn't make waves, leaving our relationship afloat atop a stagnant sea. Making nice at best keeps things as they are, but mostly only makes things worse, by not allowing them their needed illumination.

6. I'm doing the best I can.

This is perhaps the most popular excuse of all, making a mockery of accountability. Most who believe it also believe it of everyone. The notion that we are doing the best we can lets everyone off the hook, including us — for then, we don't have to ruffle any feathers, raise any hackles, kick up a storm, make a fuss, or otherwise confront anybody. Such a belief robs us of autonomy and accountability, implying as it does that we don't really have a choice as to what we do.

If we view others just as products of their conditioning, then how can we hold them responsible for what they did? After all, they couldn't help it — or could they? There's also a fear of actually recognizing that they *did* make a choice when they hurt us, for if we do see this, then what are we going to do? Can we then remain passive children in adult bodies? To move beyond such adult-erated stances, we have to stop hiding behind facile phrases like "I'm doing the best I can" or "Everyone makes mistakes" or "I'm just human." Such alibis set the bar *very* low.

When you are being unkind to your partner, and know that you are doing so, are you really doing your best? And what about when "doing our best" is simply not good enough? For example, if doing my best means that I'm remaining a drug addict and am refusing to get any treatment, then what? "I'm doing the best I can" strands us in the domain of blind compassion (neurotically tolerant, confrontation-phobic, undiscriminating "caring"), framing us as victims and enabling us to stay that way. Blind compassion (see Chapter 12) diminishes and disempowers us, whereas real compassion empowers us to take the necessary action, however painful that might be.

7. I didn't mean to hurt you.

But you did! Yes, but I didn't mean to! This claim may be accompanied by supportive claims, like "I don't know what got into me" or "I wasn't myself." Explanation and excuse indisciminately mix here, muddying what little clarity is present. If I didn't mean to hurt you, what exactly did I mean when I hurt you? And when I hurt you, was I really doing the best I could? So, so much of this is entangled with unacknowledged shame.

To untangle this, to get to its roots, we not only need to expose and illuminate our shame, but also need to separate and clearly see the various threads of self which constitute us. That in me which hurt you, and that in me which is incapable of hurting you are both inclined to refer to themselves as "I" — when what I truly am is limited to neither, and in fact *includes* both.

Yes, I am more than the "I" that hurt you, and more than the "I" that insists on not having meant to hurt you, but I am nevertheless responsible for what I allow those aspects of myself to do. When they assume the role of self — that is, when I *identify* with them — who else is responsible for that, besides me?

Even if I don't notice I've *identified* with a certain aspect or fragment of myself, I *am* responsible for my lack of awareness, just as a drunk driver is responsible, and is held responsible, for the person he hits and kills, however unaware he was of that person crossing his automotive path.

So when I hurt you and say I didn't mean to, I'm just passing the buck, *disowning* the me who did the hurting. My assignment here is blow the whistle on myself for my irresponsibility and denial, and to nondefensively receive your refusal to buy my denial — which of course undams my shame over what I've done, so that healing can occur.

8. I don't know what I'm feeling.

This is a very common statement from men during counseling work, especially when questioned by their partner as to what they're feeling. If they continue to state that they don't know what they are feeling, I usually guide them into a more precise awareness of various sensations in their body, but if they are having trouble with this, I'll sometimes ask them, "How do you know that you don't know what you're feeling?" The odds are that they either don't want to know, or won't make the effort to know.

We are always feeling something, even if it is just numbness. There is always some sort of sensation arising or lingering or passing, if only through the movements generated by our breathing.

Many, mostly men, look up or away when I ask them what they are feeling, trying to think of an answer, instead of paying attention to the here-and-now reality of their being.

"I don't know what I'm feeling" is a statement not of factuality, but of avoidance. Treat it as such.

9. An emotional affair is not really cheating.

Yes it is! If you "need" to get your deepest emotional needs met by going behind your partner's back, you are cheating on him or her, even if you don't exchange any sexual energy with your substitute partner. If you are having trouble with your partner, and you get into an emotional affair (which easily can shift into a full-blown sexual affair), you simply are betraying your partner.

Why not instead *directly* address (rather than distracting yourself from) the trouble — emotional, sexual, or whatever — which you're having with your partner, and get into some quality couples counselling? This might not be as juicy, exciting, and charged up (erotically or otherwise) as having an emotional affair, but it is far more effective and growthful, drawing us into integrity rather than away from it.

When you are with someone other than your partner, ask yourself if you'd be fine with your partner seeing exactly what you are doing at such times; if the answer is no, you are likely engaging in behavior that is as low in integrity as it is high in pleasurable exchange.

The energy you might put into an affair is precisely the energy you need to put into addressing what isn't working in your relationship.

10. Sex is supposed to make me feel better.

If we believe this — as many, mostly men, do — we easily can get quite driven about having it regularly. But why should sex have to make us feel better? What if we came to sex *already* happy, already relaxed, already open and loving and energized, instead of expecting sex to produce all this for us? We need to stop assigning sex to tasks it was not meant to do! If we, for example, are tense or anxious, why should sex have to be our outlet for our tension or anxiety?

Only when we release sex — and everything else — from the obligation to make us feel better, will we really start to feel better (see the section on sex for more on this).

11. I'll try.

Try to pick up the glass or pencil or any small object near you. If you actually picked it up, put it back down, for I didn't say to pick it up, but only to *try* to pick it up.

Trying carries within itself a counter-effort (usually in the form of inertia or self-sabotage) that ordinarily goes unnoticed or unacknowledged. That is, trying is far from a wholehearted undertaking — it is partial, emanating from only *part* of us, rather than from our core of being.

Trying is a kind of lying. It means well, and may even believe its own hype, but almost always falls short of its intented actions, simply because too much of us is simply not aligned with it. It is big on talk, and small on action — and how could it be otherwise, given how half-hearted it is?

When your partner says, "I'll try," probe deeper until their resistance to doing what they say they'll try to do surfaces. The energy locked into this resistance is the energy required to do what really needs to be done.

Take me to the bottom of your pain
Take me to the weave of your true name
Take me, take me to what you require
Take me to the heart of the fire
Let's stretch to make the leap
Let's go where love must also weep

Take me to the bottom of your pain
Take me to the weave of your true name
Take me, take me over the rise
Take me through all your goodbyes
Let's shine through our every disguise
Let's go where love has open eyes

Take me to the bottom of your pain
Take me to the weave of your true name
Take me, take me right to your core
Take me through your hidden door
Let's throw away our every alibi
Let's go where love cannot lie

Take me to the bottom of your pain
Take me to the weave of your true name
Take me, take me past your past
Take me where only the sacred will last
Let's go beyond all that binds
Let's live where insights lose their mind
Let's go where love is no longer blind

III. Working with More Difficult Stuff:

Shame, Guilt, Anger, Fear

Chapter Sixteen

SHAME: THE EXPOSURE THAT SHRINKS US

1. INTRODUCTION

Shame may be the emotion for which we have the most aversion. In a famous poll that asked what one was most afraid of, dying (as I recall) came in third or fourth, with speaking in public atop the list (speaking in public while naked was not on the list). *Mortifying.* The fear of making a fool of oneself, the fear of being humiliated, the fear of feeling full-out shame. Ultra-negative exposure.

Though shame itself is not fear, we fear it.

We may blend — and also *blanch* — shame with fear, thereby whipping up some guilt (see Chapter 17 for more on guilt), or we may push it into the background, letting other emotions take center stage. For example, if we are in a situation that triggers shame in us, we may get angry to such a convincing degree that we genuinely believe that we are *only* angry, whether our anger is directed at another or at ourself. In either case, our anger — especially if it is allowed to become *aggression* — distracts us from our shame.

Shame typically plunges us into a nastily gripping, darkly burning sense of being seriously flawed in the eyes of a convincingly critical audience, whether outer or inner. And not only does shame expose us — or at least our actions — as defective, but also emphatically deflates us in the face of such exposure, regardless of however much it heats us up.

Unlike fear and anger, shame readies us not for action, but for on-the-spot shrinkage or collapse — not necessarily full collapse, but enough to strongly *interrupt* us, to stop us in our tracks or pin us to the spot.

Shame has the power to impede what until a moment ago had been enjoyable, or at least interesting. Its signs typically are: a sudden loss of muscle tone in the neck and upper torso, so that the head slumps forward and the chest caves in; a downcasting of the eyes; an increase in the skin temperature of the face, which usually produces blushing; and a brief but intense period of confusion and disorganization.

The slump, droop, and sag of shame shows up at an early age. More than a few adults look as though they are permanently shamed — and how surprising is this, given how pervasively shaming modern culture tends to be?

It is interesting to note that shame reduces our coordination, which gives us a perhaps timely time-out or separation from our current circumstance or task, while at the same time highlighting our failure, thereby leaving us in a position where we cannot help but contrast where we were before shame kicked in and where we now are.

This contrast, at best, sobers us, so that we become less conceited, less full of ourselves, less immune to remorse, less caught up in overpursuing pleasure (and less prone to indulging in that commonplace pride that is but everted shame).

Just as disgust curbs hunger, shame curbs positive feeling.

But where disgust is a kind of "off-switch" for hunger when certain substances (like food that is going bad) or situations (like unappealing behavior) are in too-close quarters with us, shame simply reduces our level of interest in situations where just about everything else is still operating in the context of amplifying our interest. This has survival benefits, protecting us from getting too attached to maximizing our pleasures, especially when it's not safe or socially appropriate to thus indulge.

However, in its toxic forms, shame simply crushes us, making us feel like disappearing or even killing ourselves — hence *mortification.*

Shame, whether healthy or unhealthy, *shrinks* us. The commonplace labelling of psychiatrists as "shrinks" may have some of its origin in the near-inherent shame — and accompanying self-shrinkage — so many have felt when going for psychiatric help.

Probably the most neglected emotion in psychotherapy and spiritual practice is shame, even though at the same time it may be the primary emotional force animating our neuroses and spiritual ambition.

The more defective we take ourselves to be — as signalled by the presence of shame — the more driven we are likely to be to seek some sort of compensatory solution, be it narcissistic behavior, aggression, people-pleasing, withdrawal (shyness, depression, dissociation, metaphysical or spiritual escapism), hyperrationality, psychic numbing, self-deprecation, excessive interest in sexual possibility, and so on.

But let us not be too hard on shame! Without the capacity for shame, we would be devoid of conscience.

The morality of shame — and I'm speaking here of healthy shame — is responsibility. On the other hand, the morality of guilt — unhealthy shame, shame polluted with fear — is blame.

Guilt masquerades as conscience, but shame awakens or reawakens conscience. Conscience is simply the activated presence of our innate moral sense, its core of compassion arising from a mix of empathy and shame-informed — but not shame-dominated — contemplation. Moral intelligence.

What a shame it is that we so easily treat shame shamefully, even as we assign a negative connotation to being shameless! So, so much of what we do is just a strategy to avoid shame. So much shame about shame!

The key to working with shame is to meet it with compassion. This gives shame room to breathe, room to openly be itself without fear of being looked down upon.

Also, we need to differentiate shame from the fear, anger, hurt, or disgust that may arise from and camouflage it. Does the felt presence of shame drive us into compensatory emotional activity? What do we tend to do emotionally when shame is catalyzed in us? Addressing these and related questions is an essential aspect of working with shame.

Shame is painfully imbued with self-consciousness (which is a misnomer, since when we're self-conscious, we're not so much conscious of our self as we are of the other[s] apparently watching us). Becoming conscious of our self-consciousness — that is, allowing it to be the *object* rather than the *subject* of our attention — when we are in shame's grip allows us to examine our shame with at least some degree of healthy detachment.

Better yet, let's bring our shame into our heart, letting its heat branch and flush through us, while granting its message, however dark or misshapen, an audience in chambers of compassionate clarity.

Only diseased shame seeks or makes a virtue out of vengeance. Such shame, steeped in humiliation, narrows its capacity for satisfaction to the machinations of revenge; an eye-for-an-eye morality is its warcry.

If we are sufficiently shamed or humiliated, we are, in many cases, culturally sanctioned to feel justified in pursuing some kind of revenge, as is so lavishly illustrated by cinematic hero after cinematic hero enduring being shamed and then going after the villains, and the more violently the better — after all, don't the bastards deserve it? On the other hand, healthy shame aims not for vengeance against our offending others, but rather for forgiveness — not premature, shallow, token, or politically correct forgiveness, but forgiveness nonetheless, regardless of whatever consequences are deemed appropriate.

Let us cease shaming ourselves for having shame.

2. SHAME IN INTIMATE RELATIONSHIP

Intimate relationships are often pervaded by shame, but usually without much recognition that this is happening. As was explained in the first part of this chapter, shame is frequently not seen for what it is, since it tends to quickly mutate into — or get buried beneath — other states. Our aversion to feeling shame (and staying with such feeling) is so strong that most of the time our shame unfolds not as itself, but instead as aggression, withdrawal, hypercriticalness, sexual obsessiveness, excessive pride, workaholism, elitism, submissiveness, narcissicism, exaggerated competitiveness, and so on — these may appear to be very different than shame (and have an investment in appearing thus), but shame is at their root.

Shame which is not dealt with — shame that is not acknowledged, not openly felt, not directly shared, not fittingly worked with — will pollute whatever relationship in which it arises. This means that both partners need to know their history with shame in detail and inside out, and be able to recognize it for what it is *while* it is occurring. It is, for example, very, very easy to shame our partner and not realize that we are doing so — we may even, however inadvertently, shame them for their "oversensitivity" to our original shame-inducing comments and behavior. And on it goes.

I recommend that you reread the introductory section of this chapter until you can clearly see and *feel* your history with shame, shaming, and being shamed. If you are at all reluctant to do so, it may be because you have some shame around not seeing yourself more clearly. We've all got shame; our work is not to make a problem out of our shame, but to instead openly face and work with it.

When first realizing the role that shame has played in their lives, many are astonished at how pervasive, deep-cutting, and *influential* that role has been; it is as if they have discovered a lost continent of themselves, initially submerged or deeply shrouded in fog, and then illuminated by the spirit of exploration brought to it.

Shame is probably our most hidden emotion. Bringing it out of the shadows is a deeply healing undertaking, a journey that, sooner or later, we must take if we are to truly live.

Me-centered relationships are largely shame-based, with the partners having minimal awareness of the impact that shame has had — and is having — in their lives. They may, for example, be driven to excel or stand out in a particular way in order to get as far away as possible from failures which they suffered long ago, failures for which they were put down, belittled, diminished, or otherwise shamed; their pride in what they can now do is little more than everted shame, inflating them where they once were deflated.

Here, size *does* matter.

At this stage, typical reactions to shame are other-directed aggression (more common in men) and self-directed aggression (more common in women). The lone ego, unillumined and overdeveloped, usually densely or tensely masculine, rides forth all but expressionless (with only anger being allowed to show itself), six-guns righteously ablazing, sitting so tall and so rigidly erect in the saddle that the slump and droop of shame is all but impossible to detect.

And nearby, the equally unillumined but underdeveloped ego, usually feminine and more relationally-inclined than alone, nests in submissive reaction to both the blasts from the gunslinging lone ego and the critical barbs from within.

And, to thicken the mix, aggression-against-the-other and aggression-against-the-self frequently are not just overt battles, but also catalysts for shutting-down practices, like stonewalling or full withdrawal from the relationship.

Those in me-centered relationships are highly prone not only to being shamed, but also to shaming others. This can be loud and aggressive, and it can also be much more subtle, conveyed, for example, through a quick, barely perceptible rolling of the eyes. When this goes on for long enough, contempt — a toxic mix of anger and disgust — arises, signaling the disintegration of the relationship. Once we've lost respect for each other, as exemplified by the ongoing presence of contempt (and related states, like sarcasm), it's easy to reach the kind of indifference that makes reconciliation all but impossible.

We-centered relationships tend to be less shame-based, mostly because an excess of shame threatens the relationship (whereas in me-centered relationships such excess often "helps" keep the relationship in place, usually by forcing one partner into submission). At this stage, shame is, in deliberately moderate doses, often used to control and contain the relationship, through a collection of shoulds *should*-ered by both partners. Self-directed aggression is more commonplace than other-directed aggression (which is usually reserved for what is outside the relationship).

In codependent we-centered couples, denial ("It's not happening") is the usual "solution" to shame, whereas in coindependent we-centered couples, withdrawal ("I need space" or "I'm taking care of myself") is the usual "solution" to shame.

In being-centered relationships, partners do not shame each other, because they clearly see the consequences of doing so. There is no investment in putting down the other, and no drive to dominate or stand above the other. At this stage, partners are not strangers to shame's anatomy and workings; they know it well, and understand the difference between healthy and unhealthy shame.

Partners here do not let their shame mutate into aggression or relational disengagement. When they feel shame, they openly admit it. When they mess up, they don't take long to openly admit it. When they slip, they hold themselves accountable, but don't bother beating themselves up for their slippage — that is, they don't allow their shame to turn into guilt (the difference between shame and guilt is explored in the next chapter). None of this means that shame ceases to exist at this stage, but that it has shed its unhealthy forms.

At the being-centered stage of relationship, shame is simply the herald of conscience, and is consistently treated as such.

Chapter Seventeen

GUILT: ONE HAND GRABBING FOR THE CANDY, THE OTHER WIELDING A PARENTAL WHIP

1. INTRODUCTION

Guilt is little more than frozen shame, shame that has been infused with fear, manifesting as the *self-punishing* sensation of having violated some sort of contract or moral agreement.

Where shame *exposes* us, guilt *splits* us — and compensates itself for this by *continuing* to engage in whatever "bad" activity supposedly is its "can't-help-myself" raison d'être.

As such, guilt means we get to stay stuck. And *small.*

And how does guilt *split* us? It is inherently self-divisive: One aspect of us, fixatedly childish and irresponsible, does whatever it is that triggers our guilt, in conjunction with another aspect of us, fixatedly parental and authoritarian, which righteously punishes the doer of the supposed crime or misdemeanor.

The relationship between these two — basically a nastily stalemated endogenous child/parent conflict — is the essence of guilt. One hand grabbing for the candy, the other wielding a parental whip.

At the same time, however, guilt is something that *we* are doing to ourselves, something that *we* are superimposing on ourselves, something that can be counted on to keep us divided, disempowered, stuck, and exploitable.

Guilt means, among other things, that we get to *again* do whatever it is that seemingly "makes" us feel guilty — we permit ourselves to do it over and over again, even as we simultaneously punish ourselves for such transgression.

We may complain about — and even broadcast — the abuse we are suffering from our own hand and our self-incrimination, but that very punishment, if sufficiently severe, significantly *lessens* the probability of "outside" punishment (after all, who wants to beat on us when we are already doing such a good job of beating on ourselves?), while ensuring — and perhaps even, at least to some degree, *legitimizing* — our continued participation (as "victims," of course!) in what we "shouldn't" be doing.

(An example: We put ourselves down with such intensity — such self-flagellation — for watching violent porn that we not only lessen the odds of others getting on our case for watching such stuff, but also, through absorbing the very pain of our self-denigration, feel as if we've "wiped the slate clean" and are therefore justified in "treating" ourselves to once again watching violent porn.)

Guilt remains — and makes sure that it remains! — irresponsible, making impotent, self-sabotaging, or already-doomed efforts at responsibility, which it consistently confuses with blame. Its central mantra/excuse is "*I'm trying.*"

("Trying" — which features the intentionality not of us, but only of a *piece* of us — carries within itself a largely unacknowledged *oppositional* intention. For more on the nature of trying, see part 11 of Chapter 15.)

Guilt means that we get to stay small, "safely" tucked away from truly taking charge of our lives. Guilt all but ensures that we won't — and won't have to — grow up.

Guilt's prevailing reality is that of toxically simplistic right and wrong. Its moral stance is stubbornly *prerational*, dutifully skewered by the ossified finger of self-blame, self-denigration, self-castigation — anything to keep us pinned down.

The self-accusations of guilt are in the "spirit" of the other-accusations of resentment; where guilt is an amalgam of shame and fear, resentment is an amalgam of shame and aggression. In fact, one could describe resentment — especially in its globally hypercritical stance and underbelly of toxic impotence — as everted guilt.

Resentment is all about dragging others down; guilt is about dragging *ourselves* down, nailing ourselves with enough condemnation to all but guarantee our domicile in guilt, thereby stranding ourselves from any significant intimacy with responsibility and love.

Healthy shame does not take long to flush the entire system. Instead of continuing to contract us (which it does initially), healthy shame sooner or later unknots and expands us — we blush, our blood flows more freely, our body warms up, enriched with an admittedly uncomfortable yet nevertheless enlivening passion. As such, the whole body is then simply just a confession of consciously *felt* responsibility for what has happened. There is a powerful, deep-rooted impetus to coming clean, letting go, and healing, a painful yet heartfelt resolution to grow.

But guilt, on the other hand, is not really interested in healing. The guilt-ridden and guilt-spurred have little energy for genuine growth — they are driven to "do it" (that is, the thing which they feel guilty about doing) over and over again, and in order to justify "doing it" over and over again, they *have to* keep the threat of parental punishment hanging over them.

When we are stuck in guilt, we are basically just repeat offenders keeping ourselves behind bars, playing both prosecutor and accused, but without any genuine resolution, chronically resurrecting our courtroom drama and suffering the pains of once again fitting ourselves to its loveless script, while finding a "needed" (and perhaps even pleasurable) release through once again "doing it." Here, not so far below the surface, there is such grief, such a paucity of self-compassion, such an agony of desperation and addiction.

Guilt is not only a refusal to love, but also a refusal to sanely parent ourselves. In our guilt, we childishly cling to — and react to — outside parental forces which we have deeply internalized.

By contrast, healthy shame provides fertile conditions for reconnecting with the parental authority that's native to us. (For example, we have just ridiculed our partner for not being smarter in a certain area and now, through our shame — our *openly felt* shame — over having done so, take full responsibilty not only for what we've done, but also for facing and working through whatever drove us to behave in such a hurtful way in the first place.)

Shame can catalyze an environment in which genuine forgiveness can bloom; it is an opportunity to come clean and enter a truer scene. Guilt, however, works against the possibility of forgiveness.

Guilt is a flight from integrity, the very epitome of "divided we fall." The guilt-ridden are usually easy to control and exploit, for most of their power is consumed by their internal warfare.

Guilt reduces God to the ultimate parent or punishment-wielding overseer, a fact exploited by more than a few religions (as exemplified by the inculcation of the doctrine of Original Sin).

Guilt fills churches and empties hearts.

Nevertheless, guilt is not just some kind of entity at which we can or should throw darts, or which we can exorcise or exterminate. It is something that *we are doing*, something that we may not want to see that we are doing.

The very disempowerment generated by guilt empowers us to persist in it.

Guilt is false conscience.

So how to work with guilt? First of all, don't approach it with a closed heart or with moral righteousness — feeling guilty about (or shaming ourselves for) having guilt won't help!

Get in touch with the shame, fear, anger, and hurt that underlie guilt. Identify them, get detailed in your attentive survey and investigation of them, and do so as compassionately as you can. At the same time, do what you can to expand your energy, and do it as consciously as possible.

Do not let yourself automatically bounce between the childish and parental sides of guilt — recognize that neither one is *you*, but are in fact just *polarized personifications* of guilt's script.

Instead of identifying with either one, sit where you can compassionately hold both and know, right to your marrow, that you are neither.

See and feel them as clouds, and be their sky. Literally. Introduce them. Unmask them, bridge them, bring them together without taking either side, letting their mutual rainburst be your cry.

Thus do we let go of the whip, and also of the morality of blame. Thus do we shift from guilt to shame to freedom.

2. GUILT IN INTIMATE RELATIONSHIP

In me-centered relationships guilt is very difficult to work with, for a number of reasons, including the following: (1) Its basic anatomy is rarely recognized, so that its childish and parental sides remain stalemated; (2) the shame at its root is rarely seen for what it is; (3) the fear in it is only superficially dealt with, including through the release brought about by doing the "bad" thing around which guilt is constellated; and (4) the payoff for staying locked into guilt — being so stuck that expectations of us taking responsibility for ourselves are very low — is often enticing enough to keep us housed in guilt's self-punishing, bad-deed-doing domain.

When we are in guilt's clutches and upon its crutches, we get to stay small — unpleasant though this may be, we are in a position in which we don't have to grow up, which is good news for the egoity that's at the helm of me-centered relationship.

Things are not much better in codependent we-centered relationships. Guilt, if sufficiently indulged, can keep the relationship static, stagnant, stuck, "safe" — and so possesses a peculiar attraction, especially when both partners share the same guilt.

For example, they both may feel guilty about eating too much; since both are doing it (overeating and then beating themselves up for doing so, which makes them want to eat even more), and it's an in-house mutual addiction, their shared guilt keeps their relationship well-walled from the outside, however unpleasant it may be from the inside.

In coindependent we-centered relationships, there's a bit more insight into guilt, plus more resistance to embodying it. Partners here are less likely to be part of organizations that exploit the power of guilt to disempower people. They are able to bring considerable detachment to their guilt, and may even appear to be free of it, but they have only *separated* themselves from it, intellectualizing the parental side of guilt, while relegating the childish side of it to places in themselves that they rarely visit.

For example, if they overeat they usually address it with calm rationality and tolerance, while distancing themselves from the living reality of their actual habit; one hand may still be in the cookie jar, but the other has let go of the whip in favor of a more reasonable — but nonetheless still parental — approach.

Only when we reach the stage of being-centered relationship does guilt fully lose its grip on us. Both the childish and parental sides of guilt are then clearly seen, and not allowed to refer to themselves as "I." The shame and fear that constitute guilt are exposed, openly felt, and worked with, until there is no guilt, but only shame and fear, and then only available life-energy.

Those in being-centered relationships cannot be infected to any real depth by guilt; they do experience shame and fear, but don't allow these to mingle and spawn guilt.

Chapter Eighteen

ANGER: FROM REACTIVE RAGE TO WRATHFUL COMPASSION

1. INTRODUCTION

It is easy to trash anger.

After all, when it "possesses" us, are we not more prone to violence, ill will, and lovelessness? And, even if we can successfully counteract such "possession," we have, it seems, only curbed the beast — it still paces behind its bars, fanged and all too eager to do damage, while we play vigilant zookeeper. Or, less commonly, we may romanticize anger, rationalizing our "natural" urges to uninhibitedly express it, in the name of emotional de-suppression and honesty.

In both cases, however, anger is treated as though it were no more than an indwelling entity or mass, a *thing* either to be muzzled or set loose. Enthusiasts of "cooling down" and their "getting it out of our system" counterparts snipe at each other, citing — and making moral real estate out of — the dangers of either letting anger out or keeping it in. But there is much, much more to working with anger, as we shall see.

There is nothing inherently wrong with anger. Anger is not necessarily a problem, a hindrance, a sign of negativity or spiritual slippage, an avoidance of something "deeper," nor a demonstration of unlove. It is our *use* of our anger that is the real issue.

Do we blame our anger for clouding or befuddling our reason — playing victim to our passions being one of our oldest alibis — or do we assume responsibility for what we *do* with it? Do we turn our anger into a weapon, hiding our hurt behind its righteously "pumped-up" front, fueling and legitimizing our defensiveness with it, or do we instead keep it as transparent and permeable as possible, remaining non-blaming and *vulnerable* even as we allow it as full or penetrating a passion as fits the situation? Do we use our anger to get even, to score points, to overpower or outdebate, or do we use it to deepen or resuscitate our intimacy with our partner, to compassionately flame through pretense, emotional deadwood, and life-negating investments?

It's easy, in the name of angerphobia, to reject, crush, incarcerate, bad-mouth, or otherwise *violate* our anger, allowing it so few life-enhancing outlets that it — like an animal kept too long in a cage — usually behaves badly when finally released, thereby confirming our suspicions that it is indeed in need of much the same treatment as a savage beast that has somehow found its way into our house.

It is also easy, though less common, to glorify anger, with equally harmful results. Exhorting the inhibited to "get into their anger" may just lead to a forced anger, an anger of performance, an anger that leads not to healing insight, but rather to an overreliance on simplistic (and possibly aggression-reinforcing) cathartic procedures.

It is, however, not so easy to cultivate intimacy with our anger. Getting close to its heat, its flames, its redly engorged intensity, without losing touch with our basic sanity, asks much of us. But if we do not ask — and ultimately *demand* — this of ourselves, we will surely miss *knowing* not only the heat of anger's fire, but also its *light*. As much as anger can injuriously burn, it can also illuminate — it all depends on what kind of relationship with anger we choose to cultivate.

The Nature of Anger

Anger is an aroused, often heated state which combines (1) a compellingly felt sense of being wronged (hence the *moral* quality of most anger), and (2) a counteracting, *potentially* energizing feeling of power, both of which are interconnected biologically, psychologically, and culturally.

Can we identify anger — which is not a *single* emotion, but instead a family of related emotions, ranging from annoyance to rage — through the observed presence of particular behaviors? Not necessarily. We can display *none* of the behaviors supposedly characteristic of anger, and still *be* angry. Instead of pounding the table or cursing the idiot who has dared to cut us off in traffic, we may instead in our anger try even harder to please our partner, or smilingly withhold a piece of information that we know would help our partner. So can we — or others — recognize our anger through observing our behavior? Not necessarily!

Similarly, can we identify anger through the observed presence of particular feelings? Two emotions — like envy and resentment — may feel very similar, having much the same physiological characteristics, yet they do differ. We discriminate between emotions by attuning, however unknowingly, to the *context* of the situation.

Because bodily sensations are usually so obviously involved in emotion, we may confuse them with emotion itself. There is, however, more to emotion than just the feeling of it. Anger is an attitude, not just a feeling. We evaluate emotion, but not feeling — we may speak of our anger as "justified" or "unjustified," but would we speak of our feeling like vomiting as "justified" or "unjustified"?

Also, we can cease *being* angry, and yet still *feel* the very same feelings that a moment ago we identified as anger.

For example, I am raging at you for scratching my newly bought car, and suddenly I find out from a deeply trustworthy friend that you are in fact *completely* innocent of doing so, and I am now no longer angry at you. My evaluation of the situation has radically and almost instantaneously changed, yet the very feelings which I was experiencing just a moment ago — pounding heart, facial flushing, shoulders knotting, hands ready to strike — are still clearly present, having diminished only slightly.

So can I now call these feelings *angry* feelings? No, because their e*valuative* framework — or *emotional* basis — has changed.

Anger versus Aggression

Anger, contrary to popular opinion, is not necessarily the same as *aggression*. Aggression involves some form of attack, whereas anger may or may not. Aggression is devoid of compassion and vulnerability, but anger, however fiery its delivery might be or might have to be, *can* be part of an act of caring and vulnerability. Nevertheless, anger in general remains all but synonymous with aggression.

Aggression is not so much an outcome of anger, as an *avoidance* of it and its underlying feelings of woundedness and vulnerability. Recognizing this is essential for relational depth and maturity.

Viewing anger as aggression — or as the cause of aggression — gives us an excuse to classify it is a "lower" or "primitive" emotion. Or something far from spiritual. But anger is far from "primitive," though what we *do* with it may be far from civilized!

Rejected anger easily mutates into aggression, whether active or passive, other-directed or inner-directed. Thus does a means of communication become a means of weaponry.

Anger assigned to do injury, however subtly, is not really anger, but *hostility*. Anger that masks its own hurt and vulnerability is not really anger, but hardheartedness or hatred in the making, seeking not power *with*, but power *over*.

However, there is a potential healing here: to *reverse* the equation, to convert aggression, hostility, hatred, and every other diseased offspring of mishandled anger *back into* anger.

This conversion, however, does not mean eviscerating or drugging the energy of such negative states, but rather liberating it from its life-negating viewpoints, so that its intensity and passion can coexist with a caring, significantly awakened attention. In this sense, the world needs not less anger, but *more*. Especially anger coming from the heart.

Violence — the brass knuckles of abused wounds — ignores, tramples or dynamites personal boundaries, but anger, in many cases, *protects* or *guards* such boundaries, at best resolutely exposing and illuminating (or perhaps even flaming through) barriers to intimacy or integrity, *without* abusing those who are maintaining such barriers. Anger that burns cleanly leaves no smoldering pockets of resentment or ill-will.

Violence is *not* a result of anger, but is an abuse or *violation* of anger.

Working with Anger: Four Approaches

The four approaches to working with anger introduced below provide a framework not only capable of making sense out of the diverse, complex, and enormous amount of material concerning anger, but also sufficiently inclusive to cover both personal *and* transpersonal considerations of anger.

(1) **Anger-In** refers to strategies favoring the restraining and redirection of the energies characteristic of raw anger. Not surprisingly, advocates of this approach emphasize the importance of *not* directly expressing anger. Self-control, subduing and recontextualizing our anger — these are the cornerstones of anger-in. Anger-in "experts" tend to equate the expressing of anger with "venting," a lack of self-control, violence, and aggression. Anger-in practices teach us not only to identify those perceptions and interpretations that catalyze anger, but also relaxation

and cooling-off techniques. Reinterpreting supposed provocations is essential to anger-in; such reappraisal reduces the probability of anger being openly expressed by removing or at least shrinking the perception of being under attack.

Though anger-in may make too much of a virtue out of controlling, managing, and non-angrily "expressing" anger, it does make a strong case for learning to step back from anger so that its more extreme or irrational impulses can be reconsidered or given more contextual space. Nevertheless, anger-in has a difficult question before it: How successful can a way of working with anger be that does not include openly expressing the actual feelings of anger? Would we, by analogy, consider a grief therapy to be successful that did not include the actual expression of grief?

(2) **Anger-Out** refers to approaches that emphasize the importance of directly and fully expressing the energies and intentions of anger. At the very core of anger-out theory and work is the notion of catharsis, which remains a controversial topic in therapeutic practice, despite evidence that incorporating catharsis in anger-management work makes it more effective.

Advocates of anger-out say that suppressed anger is not healthy — better to bring it to the surface (or "dig it up") and release/express it, they claim. As appealing and apparently medically sound as such "down-to-earth" logic may be, it can tend to overemphasize a merely *physical* approach to anger, as if anger was just something to discharge or eliminate from the body. The emotional-release work that characterizes anger-out practices can range from enthused licence to blindly cut loose (or irresponsibly "act out" anger) to profoundly healing, integration-promoting release and illumination.

(3) **Mindfully Held Anger** refers to approaches in which anger is consciously contained, not emotionally expressed, and meditatively attended to, with a key intention being neither to suppress anger nor

act it out. In its emphasis on neither repressing nor acting out emotion, this approach appears to offer a solution to the anger-in/anger-out dichotomy. In being wakefully present with our anger, thereby closely witnessing the actual *process* of it (in its feeling, cognitive, perceptual, and social dimensions), we also bear witness, at least to some degree, to the very "I" who is busy being angry. That is, our perspective shifts from how angry we feel to *who it is* who feels it. We then take good care of our anger, cradling it much like we would an upset child.

At its best, the mindful holding of anger is not so much a containment of anger as a deliberately *intimate* embracing and investigation of it, a willingness to stay with our anger without outwardly expressing it. Through such loving alertness, anger can be transformed into the energy of understanding and compassion. However, this practice carries its own dangers — as suggested by the more negative connotations of the term "holding" — especially when it is engaged in prematurely or in order to flee or suppress anger, as when we are not so much sitting *with* our anger as *on* it.

(4) **Heart-Anger** refers to approaches in which openly expressed anger and compassion consciously and beneficially coexist. Put together the virtues of anger-in, anger-out, and mindfully held anger — healthy rationality and restraint, emotional openness and authenticity, meditative openness and compassion — and minimize the difficulties associated with each, and heart-anger emerges.

Heart-anger is anchored both in full-blooded aliveness and in clear caring for the other. As fierce as it sometimes can be (or has to be), heart-anger is but the emissary of wrathful compassion. Here, the expression of anger is not necessarily rethought or kept to oneself, nor always given free rein, but rather is deliberately infused with wakeful, investigative attention, without any requisite dilution or non-expression of its passion. It is "clean" anger, incisive, non-blaming, mindful, contextually sensitive, heated yet illuminating — rooted in both the personal and the transpersonal.

As such, it could be called *soul-centered* anger (by *soul*, I mean that depth of individuality in which egoity is clearly and functionally peripheral to Being). Such anger has a broad enough sense of human suffering to embrace a radically inclusive morality; it possesses sufficient faith in Life to persist in its fierce caring; and it has the guts to carry all this out.

If all that was necessary was that it shine, heart-anger surely would, but it knows that it often must also burn. And, because of this, it knows that it must also weep.

2. ANGER IN RELATIONAL STAGES

In me-centered relationships, anger-in is mostly just repression, and anger-out mostly just indulgence. There is no mindfully held anger, nor any heart-anger. Anger here is all but indistinguishable from aggression (whether active or passive). Fighting dirty is rarely seen as fighting dirty, except when it is clearly violent. At this stage, anger is sentenced to hard labor in the service of being right. It also, especially in men, may be employed not only to police boundaries, but also to expand them in opportunistic or imperialistic fashion. If all this sounds primitive, it's because it is — egocentricity rules here, whatever its IQ.

In we-centered codependent relationships, things are not much better. There is a little more awareness of anger, and much less of a tendency to let it become aggression, but there is no more than the faintest trace of mindfully held anger and heart-anger. Aggression is primarily passive, at least within the relationship. Anger-in is strongly favored over anger-out. Heated or passionate anger is mostly viewed, and judged, as just a loss of control. Unlike in me-centered relationships, anger is used here to guard the relationship itself from outside influences.

In we-centered coindependent relationships, anger-in is still the preferred approach, with anger-out used only occasionally. Mindfully held anger is also sometimes employed. Heart-anger is just as rare as in the previous stage. Aggression is primarily intellectual, and is often recognized as such. Anger is not only used here to guard the relationship from outside influences, but also to guard the independence of both partners within the relationship. Anger is perhaps at its most civil at this stage, but such civility is, unlike in me-centered codependent relationships, sometimes challenged. There is a yearning for deeper, more life-giving ways of dealing with anger, but energy and attention are only sporadically invested in such yearning.

In being-centered relationships, anger is an *ally*. Mindfully-held anger and heart-anger usually predominate over anger-in and anger-out. Aggression, if it manifests at all, is immediately recognized and quickly translated back into anger. Partners here don't bicker or indulge in go-nowhere arguments when they are angry, but instead express their anger to each other openly and passionately, and with enough care to ensure that things get resolved without delay. Their anger and their love coexist to enough of a degree so that they can allow each other some messiness in the initial expressing of their anger (which sometimes is needed to get it flowing).

Anger in a being-centered relationship can be skillfully contained, and just as skillfully de-contained. Reactive anger, whether active or passive, has now become but wrathful compassion.

3. GETTING CLOSER TO ANGER

Anger is moral fire. Whether it is destructive or constructive is in our hands. And our hearts. In the fiery care of clean anger, passion and compassion coexist, as do heat and light. We need to respect our anger, to cease viewing it as a problem, spiritual hindrance, or something beneath us, so that it might serve our well-being.

Neither to repress nor to indulge in our anger is far from easy, asking, among other things, that we meet it with genuine caring. Anger that is denied compassion easily becomes anger that is delivered, however indirectly, without compassion.

But how to bring compassion to anger? First of all, we need to approach it without aversion, which means becoming more *intimate* with whatever aversion we might have toward anger. Moving toward what we typically move away from in ourselves can be very liberating. The degree of caring with which we approach our anger is the degree of caring with which we can infuse the anger we give to others.

Rage that does not violate — this is the fiery face of compassion, the wrathful shout of the awakening heart.

The exploration of anger ought not to be the occupation of just a few. Not to explore anger, not to be intimate with it, is a dangerous choice, leaving us cut off from the very forcefulness and energetic underlining that may *already* be enlisted in the service of aggression, hatred, and mean-spiritedness. Not to know our anger is to keep ourselves in the dark, and in danger of being violent instead of simply angry.

Openly acknowledging and unguardedly experiencing our anger — both as an unfolding process and as direct expressiveness in the vulnerable raw — makes it less of an "it" and more reclaimed *us*.

At its best, anger — heart-including, open-bellied, open-throated, and so, so passionately *alive* — cannot help but support love and integrity, for it is then deeply connected to need, to vulnerability, to bareness of soul. It is then but *relational fire*, helping to both clear and light our way into an ever deeper intimacy, an intimacy that ultimately includes all that we are.

The fiery intensity at the heart of anger asks not for smothering, spiritual rehabilitation, nor mere discharge, but rather for a mindful embrace that does not necessarily require any dilution of passion, any lowering of the heat, nor any muting of the essential voice in the flames.

Bringing our anger into our heart is not only an act of love for ourselves, but for all beings, since such a practice increases the odds that we will not let our anger mutate into aggressiveness, hostility, and hatred, but rather into compassion-centered activity.

In no longer abandoning or destructively harnessing our anger, we move a step closer to being and standing up for the very love that we most desire from others.

Anger *can* be love — may we permit it to be so.

4. ANGER & RELATIONAL INTIMACY

Anger can obstruct, erode, or even demolish relational intimacy. And anger can also enhance it. As much as anger's fire can injuriously slash and burn, it can also illuminate and heal — it all depends on what kind of relationship with anger we choose to cultivate.

Relationships stuck in anger-fueled power struggles are often sustained by a mutual bargaining (for example: "I won't complain about your drinking if you'll stop trying to have sex with me so often"). Far-from-sacred contracts these are, simply being ways to maintain the status quo, to take care of business.

To go beyond treating relationship as business or as something merely to negotiate or manipulate one's way through, both partners need to be committed to uncovering, exploring, and awakening from their neurotic rituals, including those which are anger-based, anger-infused, anger-catalyzing, and otherwise anger-related.

This necessitates a responsibly expressed, timely sharing of our inner workings — including our resistance to doing so! — regarding our anger, whether we're in the mood to do so or not. Our anger then is not necessarily kept to ourselves, nor disguised or muted, nor reduced to an angerless report, but is — under appropriate conditions — openly shown and shared, not just as content, but also, to varying degrees, as energy, raw energy.

This point, where we in most cases would probably just trot out our usual roles — the misunderstood one, the victim, the reasonable one, the doormat, the one with the "more mature" way of expressing anger, and so on — is precisely where even a trace of wakefulness is of immense use, so as to inwardly acknowledge not only our state, but also the degree of our *identification* with that state.

When a mutually compassionate eye can be cast upon the highlighted reactivity of one or both partners, the relationship is on course.

The heat of our preferences — how easily and quickly they can stir up anger, while our mind, apparently uninvited, tosses in commentary: Should I take my anger seriously? Should I wait until it passes? Should I express it directly, right now, or should I maybe reword it a little? Why is this happening to me? It is definitely *your* fault this time — why shouldn't I be angry at you? I guess my spiritual practice isn't what I thought — but would I be getting angry if you were treating me better? Observe the sensations and the intentions, inhale, exhale, inhale, exhale, inhale — damn, this just is not working! I promised myself I wouldn't lose control again, and here I am, already losing it — which would not be happening if you hadn't done what you just did, right? And so on. Under such conditions, our thoughts are but kerosene.

Where there are judgments (whether directed at others or at ourselves), there is going to be anger. This does not mean that we ought somehow to get rid of our judgments — a bound-to-fail task, so long as we have a mind! — but rather that we keep them in healthy perspective, mining them for whatever nuggets of insight or intuition they might possibly contain, amidst all their noise and fuss and devotion to negative evaluation.

Relational intimacy can catalyze the surfacing of judgments and reactive tendencies that might have otherwise gone undetected. We can mask such judgments, but we cannot completely conceal their presence. The feeling and delivery of our judgmentalness may easily cut into our partner, generating hurt, distance, confusion, and fear — unless we can quickly, honestly, and with at least some caring, share the actual feelings housed at the hub of our judgmentalness, including those for which we have the most aversion, like anger.

It is not uncommon to be angry at our anger ("When will I be free of this damn anger?"), rejecting of it ("I shouldn't be angry!"), or simply disconnected from it ("You may think that I am, but I'm *not* angry!"). However, instead of fighting or fleeing our anger, we need to become more deeply acquainted with it — but how can we do this if we will only examine our anger from a distance (anger-in), or insist on emptying ourselves of its energies when it arises (anger-out)?

Intimacy with our anger, and anger in general, enhances self-knowledge, integrity, relational depth, and spiritual maturation, helping us to embody a passion as potently alive as it is responsible, as we learn the art of being angry with an open — or committed-to-being-open — heart.

Gender and Anger in Intimacy

The disempowerment of women has, among other things, meant the suppression and devaluation of their anger. Where male anger, despite anger's supposedly "lower" origins, has in many circumstances — war, contact sports, vigilante heroics — often been viewed as healthy, morally justified, or even ennobling, female anger has generally been viewed far less favorably, as illustrated by our less-than-flattering labels for angry women. He's assertive, hotheaded, pissed off, just letting off some steam, taking care of business; she, on the other hand, is just a nag or bitch.

Thus have anger-in or anger-suppressing practices tended to be more expected of women than of men. Anger is culturally held as far less legitimate an expression for women than for men. The result is that for many women anger is largely unavailable as a *resource*.

A woman marooned from her own anger is likely going to have a harder time maintaining healthy boundaries; she may feel more helpless, more fearful, more prone to despair and depression. When her anger cannot be depressed — that is, kept or *pressed* down — its energies may be routed into resentment or bitterness. And what a pity this is, given that anger can be, including in its fieriness, a form of *caring*. In my work I have often seen a woman's rage — full-out, clean rage — cut through the cognitive muddling of her partner or other men, waking them up to what they're actually doing.

For anger to be a resource in relationship requires not only that it be permitted its innate vulnerability, but that it also be valued, and valued equally, in both women and men. So long as female anger is treated as something less worthy of respect than male anger, relational approaches to anger will remain superficial or unproductive.

Anger asks not for domestication, but for an *honoring* of its wildness, a receptive, suitably expressive outlet for its elemental, primally alive nature. Unfortunately, the wildness in men often tends to be either crushed or channeled into mere savagery (however sophisticated), and the wildness in women just as often tends to be smothered, reduced to various forms of nagging, or trivialized as mere bitchiness.

Women have been much more subject to domestication and niceness implants than have men, and yet I have observed again and again that heart-anger usually comes more readily to women than to men. A possible reason for this is that women generally are more willing to bring some caring into their anger, whereas men are typically more prone to converting their anger into aggression.

There is more to this, however. The active/dynamic (or going-toward) capacity commonly attributed to men, in contrast to the corresponding passive/receptive (or taking-in) capacity commonly attributed to women, may have some truth in certain areas, but not very much at all when it comes to psychological/emotional life. Much of marriage counselling deals with the far more active roles that women generally take — for better or for worse — with regard to the interior life of their relationship. Thus it is no surprise that women would tend to be more accessible to heart-anger, since they are, in general, already more inclined toward both caring and taking an active or even challenging role in the arena of psychological/emotional communication.

A woman's impassioned and resolute shaking up of the relational status quo — disturbing the man's complacency or supposed expertise — can be a potent awakening agent. And vice versa. Anger and love can exist at the same time in a mature relationship!

Essential to relational intimacy is a "level playing field" between men and women, the establishing of which asks for more than political correctness or token egalitarianism. In looking at anger in the context of intimate relationship, we need to take into account not only the fact that genuine intimacy between men and women is a very recent phenomenon ("Marriage," quips family therapist Carl Whitaker, "is when families exchange hostages") — given that such intimacy requires being-to-being equality — but also the cultural suppression and devaluing of female anger.

"Let's try to work this out rationally," says one partner (more often than not the man) during a couples counselling session, trying to confine relational anger to a merely intellectual exchange. Breaking into apparent rationality — especially emotionally disconnected rationality — is a very common practice among men when they are faced with their partner's anger. Such a choice may not be so much an embracing of logic as it is an act of fear, deflection, or even terror.

During couples' work, I have often seen women become more present and alive — and sometimes even *relieved* — when their partners have *directly* expressed anger to them. However, when the situation has been reversed, I have noticed that the men usually pull back, blanch, become numb, or go blank, perhaps finding some refuge or "protection" in disembodied rationality, sudden interest in what's on the carpet or the ceiling, apparent deafness, or — especially — "courtroom" tactics designed to turn the critical finger back at the woman (as in "reasonably" shifting the focus to flaws, real or imagined, in her delivery or content).

This tendency for male withdrawal from anger-infused engagement can be partially explained by research findings that men are inclined to be more physiologically overwhelmed — or "flooded" — than women by outright marital confrontation, at least in counselling situations. (Other research, though, indicates that women usually show greater physiological responsiveness to marital difficulty and distance than men, perhaps because they tend to be more sensitive to the erosion of intimacy.)

Most men, however, don't become flooded when their wives "stonewall" (or stonily and noncommunicatively disengage from any meaningful interaction with them), probably because it is less threatening to them than actual confrontation. Women, however, become flooded — their heart rates going up dramatically — when being stonewalled by their husbands. Her anger may or may not be in the service of intimacy, but his stonewalling (most stonewallers are men) is definitely not, since it all but completely severs the possibility of working out conflicts.

This does not mean, however, that men ought to abdicate, mute, or eviscerate their own power and become unquestioning receptacles for female anger, but rather that they learn to meet it (assuming that it's not abusive) *nondefensively* — especially in the spirit of heart-anger — so that they might really listen to it and respond in fitting fashion.

A man may have trouble hearing what his partner is saying when she is angry at him (and vice versa!), perhaps because he is so busy feeling threatened or overwhelmed. Hearing her anger — including the issues it is attempting to underline or address — might begin with a simple acknowledgment of his fear, upset, or mistrust, shared in a manner that invites further exploration. (See the earlier chapters on Reactivity and Emotional Illiteracy.)

Also crucial to such hearing is the need to cut through any assumptions that frame the listener as an underling. If we assume that the act of listening closely to another — especially when they are critical of us or angry at us — puts us in a subordinate position, we may, particularly as men, try to reassert our presumed status or autonomy by challenging our partner's authority, even when such challenge is clearly inappropriate or just plain stupid.

If we won't listen — and if we still tend to associate listening with being female — we won't find much intimacy, regardless of our efforts to power our way into it. Not surprisingly, the imagery of intimacy (especially in its softer, more tender and receptive dimensions) has been far less honored historically than the imagery of warriorhood.

Imagine a new image: The warrior of intimacy, female or male, who can give anger with full-blooded yet compassionate and vulnerable intensity, and who can also receive anger — not absorbing or swallowing it, nor playing martyred target for it, but simply responding to it nondefensively, letting it in not like an invader but like a *guest*.

Making Room for Reactive Anger

To get to the non-reactive (that is, conscious and responsible) expression of anger, we may need to begin by making room, compassionate and skillfully structured room, for the reactive "unleashing" of anger, if only in suitable therapy chambers. (What I am saying here, though in opposition to anger-in stands, is *not* a stamp of approval for anger-out and its often simplistic advocacy of mere energetic discharge.)

Pushing away, drugging, incarcerating, or trying to think away our emotional reactivity — whether it is overheated or frozen — does not eradicate it. We can sedate it with distractions or countering thoughts, or attempt to replace it with more socially acceptable behavioral skills, but in so doing — and sometimes we may need to do so, as when we are so fragile or shaky that sedation of some form is necessary — we are basically engaged in not much more than trying to force it into submission.

The point is thus not to "civilize" our emotional reactivity — which may be not an irrationality of the feeling itself, but of its prevailing mode of expression — but rather to provide it with conditions through which it can be, however gradually, liberated from its viewpoint without robbing it of its passion. After all, how can we expect it to behave responsibly when we deny it light, love, a compassionate ear, and the room to breathe freely?

So anger *sometimes* may need to be expressed uncleanly at first. This is *not* advocacy of "anything goes" anger-out license, but rather a *brief* yet substantial tolerance for the sort of anger that is initially messy in its delivery. Foundational to this is a safe "container," such as that of good psychotherapy or a relatively mature relationship (we-centered coindependent or being-centered).

If we expect our (and our partner's) anger to be "clean" — that is, mindful, vulnerable, responsible, and non-blaming — *right away*, we are pressuring ourselves (and our partner) with unrealistic expectations.

Once reactive anger has been allowed to break loose and speak freely in a safe, skillfully overseen environment — wherein rationality, raw feeling, and mindfulness are simultaneously honored — it quickly mutates, with perhaps a firm reminder or two, into a non-blaming, vulnerable, yet still powerfully alive anger, an anger that comes as much from the heart as from the belly and head.

Such anger-release — or anger-exposure — is not a performance, but a process that may need to be messy or somewhat chaotic initially, so as to provide a starting point for its deeper rhythms and outpourings.

This is not an excuse for irresponsibility, but rather a reminder that approaching anger with caring instead of aversion can catalyze a deep healing, a healing wherein emotional reactivity is not so much declawed and domesticated as it is illuminated and permitted to metamorphose into something more life-giving and therefore relationship-enhancing.

Expressing and Receiving Anger

Brian and Tina are at a stalemate. Both are articulate and insightful, yet they are stuck. Their knowledge — both are therapists — does not seem to be making any difference. He wants more commitment from her, she wants less pressure from him, and both are unhappy. She says she feels guilty about her lack of commitment to being with him, so we talk about her guilt and its roots, but still there is little life in the room.

They are both clearly angry and very much under control — firmly in position, armed in their attempted openness, trying to be non-combative in their combativeness. The stage is set.

"Face each other," I say, "and keep eye contact." Tina briefly raises her hands slightly, palms out, smiles, and delivers some more dead-end insight. "Do that again with your hands," I say, "and breathe deeper." She grins. I see a flash of shame. Her hands are sliding up and down the outside of her thighs. "What do your hands want to do?" I ask her.

In an instant, her hands are on Brian's knees, pushing him back. Immediately, she pulls back, smiling, changing the subject. I ask her what she's feeling as she smiles, and she says that she's angry, and that she's withdrawing from him. Tension fills the room. We briefly talk about how easily she puts herself down for not wanting to be closer to him; even to directly give him her anger would be, she says, a kind of giving in. And so on. Brian is hurt, but still present.

"Let's try a different tack," I suggest. "Tina, I want you to express your anger to Brian as fully as possible, but without any words." She no longer can smile. I have her hold her a pillow between her hands, to be squeezed as hard as she can. A half minute or so passes. I can see and feel her rage, but she is silent. I ask her where she is most tense, and she says her throat and jaw.

Suddenly, she leans forward, screaming at him, her sounds deep and powerful; she is clearly not acting. Brian now looks much more awake — and caring. Tina is full-blooded in what she is allowing, and is simultaneously very vulnerable. Tears mix with her rage. Less than a minute later, I have her interlock hands with him while she bites down on a towel that I pull on; this loosens her jaw and neck. For a minute or so, she pushes against him, biting very hard, her eyes pure fury and hurt. Then I have her let go of the towel and his hands. Silence, and a deeper silence.

Both had complained of not having enough of a soul-connection, but now it is evident that they are plugged into a very real intimacy. He, unlike many men, did not pull back or "disappear" in the face of her raw anger. They are not through their difficulty, but are now in a place where they are far more capable of getting through it.

The expression of anger and the need to take action are not necessarily the same thing. The direct expression of anger-energy is simply an act of exposure, whereas the need to have events go this way or that has more to do with power and control.

Restricting anger expression to verbal combat only keeps it from being as healing a process as it could be if it were to also — under the right conditions — to *include* the nonverbal expression of undisguised and uncensored anger (as illustrated in the vignette above).

When anger is "uncaged" in a suitable environment at the right time, it often will, after a minute or two of full-throated, full-bodied release, be accompanied by fitting words and phrasings that potently articulate the heart of the matter. Thus can skillfully steered anger-out become more than venting, more than a merely eliminative strategy, eventually mutating, to a significant degree, into heart-anger.

In a relatively awakened relationship, the actual intent of our anger can, at least some of the time, be safely verbalized, openly and specifically. At times — if there is enough trust, love, and mindfulness — the confession of such intent may need to be also physically expressed (as when anger is particularly intense, edgy, or gripping) through wringing a towel, pounding a pillow or sofa, or engaging in other similarly nondestructive expressions of such energy.

Sometimes, in the presence of sufficient maturity and mutual caring, we can openly confess the intent of our more aggressive urges — an honest verbalization of such intent, if vulnerably expressed, will very quickly defuse it, radically lessening our desire to act it out.

To expose our darker reactive intentions with clarity, vulnerability, and perhaps some degree of dramatic exaggeration, can be, even though it might appear otherwise, an act of love, providing an illuminating — and valuable — inside look at our uglier urges, soul-crushing habits, core wounds, and their attending anger.

Openly sharing what we are ashamed or afraid of in ourselves makes us not only more intimate with such qualities, but also with each other.

Even so, we may still go to great lengths to avoid exposing or sharing not only the more shameful or embarrassing imperatives of our anger, but also its *passion*. Getting righteous during our anger may be pointless, but no more so than submitting to our partner's demands (tacit or not) that we: (1) not get openly angry; (2) spare them such raw intensity; (3) prove (through suffocating, sterilizing, or at least muting our anger) that we are loving; and (4) in short, let them in this particular situation remain in control, "safely" removed from the heat of our anger.

If we are on the receiving end of anger coming from our partner, particularly heated or wide-open anger, it may be very tempting to deny them significant access to us, even if their anger is being delivered cleanly. We may interrupt, deflect, minimize, or try to detour their intensity of feeling (and/or content), perhaps informing them that they are out of control or behaving irresponsibly, saying to them in so many words, "Can't we do this another way?"

This apparently reasonable request, however appropriate it might be at times (as when the environment is not sufficiently supportive of an "uncivilized" exchange, or when anger is being abusively expressed), is usually an avoidance of anger, as well as a confession of not being intimate with our own anger. That is, if we don't successfully defuse or mute our partner's anger at us, it might catalyze our own anger into a more active form, and the more opposed we are to this, the more we will tend to oppose, obstruct, or sabotage our partner's direct expression of anger.

We may even — without raising our voice, of course! — demand from them in the midst of their anger that they demonstrate that they do indeed love us. To do so may mean that they have to cease being angry (or at least *looking* angry), given that our prevailing model of love very likely does not include an angry-faced or wrathful love. If anger signals the end or absence of love for us — as it might have in our past — then we are going to have a strong investment in suppressing it, both in ourselves and in others, stranding ourselves from the realization that anger and love can both exist at the same time.

Looking for proof that our angry other is not rejecting us can quite easily obscure the fact that *we* may be rejecting them and their anger. Demanding that they show us love (in the way that we think love ought to look) while they are being angry at us can quite easily obscure the realization that we may not be loving them during their exposure of their anger — we might even be, however unwittingly, *punishing* them for being angry at us.

Our "calm" or "rational" or "spiritual" withdrawal from them when they are angry at us is likely not an act of real caring, but rather one of fear, aversion, or passive aggression.

It is easy to make a virtue out of withheld anger, but such withholding may be just another form of anger.

Part of our difficulty here may be that we are still confusing anger with aggression, forgetting that taking the aggression out of anger allows for an anger that helps *protect* a couple's intimacy. Aggressive behavior is anger gone awry, anger that has been stripped of its vulnerability and capacity to serve relational deepening and intimacy.

The quality of awareness central to the practice of mindfully held anger is indispensable here. If we, as receivers of our partner's anger, can through such practice lessen or even cease our identification with what such anger is trying to address in us, then we can, in a sense, stand *beside* our partner, looking with him or her at what he or she is angry about, with minimal reactivity or defensiveness.

In so doing, we are openly hearing both our partner's anger and our response to it, while remaining compassionately aware of the overall situation. This allows us to realize, and not only intellectually, that our partner's anger is not actually at us, but at what we have been or are *doing*. To be mindful here does not necessarily mean or require the non-expression of anger — at best, it coexists with both compassion and unshackled aliveness.

For anger to enhance intimacy, it needs to be met with nondefensive, empathetic listening (which does not necessarily mean that the partner listening should suppress his or her own anger!), listening in which agreement or disagreement with what is being said or conveyed remains *secondary* to our empathy and caring for the other. Such is the essence of receiving anger.

Rejecting our partner's anger — not aggression, but *anger* — simply short-circuits it. This generally encourages the stockpiling of anger-energy and frustration, along with a resulting pressure to find other outlets, such as the subtle cruelties of passive aggression.

Anger that is rejected, anger that is denied compassion, anger that is vilified or ostracized or declawed, is the very anger that corrodes and sabotages intimacy.

Rejected anger, anger denied its natural or needed expression, does not necessarily vanish. To take but one example, such anger may — like toothpaste in a tube that's being tightly gripped at its "waist" — be rerouted "upward" and recruited for intellectual aggression, and it may also be (particularly in men) squeezed "downward" into the pelvic "bowl" for drainage and/or dramatization through masturbation, pornographic proclivity, erotic violence, and the more "civilized" variations of these that often pass for "normal" sex.

Men who ejaculate away the energy and thrust of their anger — emptying it into their partner — are simply forcing their sexuality to be the outlet, and their partner the outhouse, for their anger. When we assign sex to stress-release (thereby refusing to release sex from the obligation to make us feel better), we are doing little more than screwing ourselves, marooning ourselves from real intimacy.

Sharing anger in an intimate relationship does not always have to remain a serious affair. Playfulness and healthy anger expression are not mutually exclusive. Skillful teasing in the midst of anger may in fact create *more* room for hearing what is really being said, testing the health and resiliency of our edges, keeping us fluid, even if our bones are brittle with age. Such teasing is the leavening of healthy criticism. It puts down our sweaty fretting and fussing without putting us down.

The joy that can sometimes arise during full-out anger is not necessarily a sign of aberration, but may instead simply signal the sheer pleasure of being full-bloodedly and unabashedly alive (not to mention the sudden and expansive intrusion of deeper perspectives, however brief).

In such a richly embodied totality of expressiveness, there might be unexpected openings to far-from angry states. Anger at its raging peak can, for example, sometimes mutate almost instantaneously into deep joy or prayerful gratitude.

At such times, the daimonic power of anger — "daimonic" meaning any natural function (anger, lust, grief, ecstasy) having the power to take over us — literally possesses us, making of us a "clearing" into which deeper dimensions of being can nakedly show themselves.

In the thundering heat of intense anger, a happy-to-be-alive feeling may thus sometimes emerge — especially when deep intimacy and trust are present. Some signs of anger may still linger, but there will also be a deep and natural empathy, plus a spaciousness which allows integrity to surface, tears to stream freely, humor to upstage righteousness, and love to shine bright.

When anger and love are permitted to coexist — as happens most commonly in being-centered relationships — intimacy cannot help but deepen.

Anger does not disappear as we awaken, and in fact may become even more fiery, but burns cleanly, serving the well-being of all involved.

Chapter Nineteen

FEAR: APPREHENSIVE SELF-CONTRACTION

1. INTRODUCTION

As simplistic as it may sound, fear often is just excitement in drag. If we are excited and then we contract, fear arises; if we are fearful and then expand, excitement arises. Same energy, different context.

This is not all that difficult to recognize when we consider our fear in its physical/physiological dimensions, but not so easy to recognize when we consider our fear in its mental dimensions. (Later in this chapter, doubt, which is largely a cognitive kind of fear, will be explored in detail.)

Fear and anger are biochemically all but identical. Same adrenaline, different intention and directionality. When the fearful get angry, they are not afraid any more, but just angry. Not that getting angry is the solution for fearfulness — but the arising of anger can really *empower* us, in contrast to the arising of fear.

Fear comes in many forms — worry, anxiety, panic, paranoia, angst, terror, dread, doubt — but fundamentally is just apprehensive self-constriction, a contractile aversion that takes shape as a mildly to deeply unpleasant gripping feeling that announces, compellingly and viscerally: *I am not safe;* or *I am threatened;* or *I am in danger.*

This message — scrawled in our own blood — may often be impervious to cognitive intervention. Consider the following example: If we suffered a particularly difficult birth, with our vital signs having accelerated for a significant amount of time into zones of extreme danger — so that our biological *survival* was clearly at stake — we obviously didn't mentally reflect on our situation (our brain not being developmentally capable of doing so), but rather *automatically* reacted by "doing" whatever most quickly and effectively reduced the danger, like going neurologically limp or "depressing" our vital signs.

Later in life, when in the presence of danger (real or imagined), we may then not only get afraid, but may also revert, beyond any mental counter-effort, to what originally had "worked" to save our life — withdrawing, shutting down, turning off, getting depressed, whatever does the job. Many relationships are ruined or kept in the shallows by such reversion (which is not always a result of birth trauma!) — the "depressing" of our vitals signs both "saves" and destroys us, making us all but incapable of sustained intimacy.

However it manifests, fear very easily undercuts our rationality. Fear that's allowed to infiltrate our mind doesn't waste any time generating thoughts that support and amplify it.

Animals get afraid — demonstrating the physiology and characteristic behaviors of fear — when *actual* danger is present and registers; the electrifying biochemistry of fear immediately enables them to flee or, less commonly, to freeze.

Humans, however, are usually far less practically inclined, at least after infancy, getting afraid not only in the present, but also projecting fearfulness into the past (as in guilt, which is shame injected with fear) and the future (as in worry or anxiety), generally keeping ourselves not only chronically afraid, but also overcommitted or enslaved to whatever most successfully keeps us sufficiently distanced from our fear.

Fear can be adaptive or maladaptive. The rush of fear we feel when we are getting too close to a precipice is useful, immediately alerting and readying us for needed action (like stepping back). Worry, on the other hand, is far from useful — when we permit it to gnaw at us, and to enlist our cognition in its service, we're only keeping ourselves off track, bound up in a too narrowly framed view. Worry — which is but socially acceptable anxiety — keeps us spinning in a cranial cramp, until we leave for more life-giving territory (perhaps after having "worried our head off").

To journey into, unguardedly feel, and directly relate *to* our fear (instead of *from* it) requires that our usual distancing strategies, cognitive and otherwise, be exposed and disarmed — assuming, of course, that it is timely to do so. Our fear can then be touched and known from the inside, and eventually divested of its power to shrink, misguide, or intimidate us.

Our smaller fears, unpleasant as they might be, are not usually very difficult to temporarily escape or sedate — we know what we are afraid of; we are perhaps even oddly comforted by its uncomfortable or edgy familiarity; and we know when to throw it a piece of meat and when not to. We know it well enough to know how to take the edge off it, through positive thinking, sex, food, drugs, intense exercise, electronic fixes, and other such distracting preoccupations — we know where the corral is, how high a fence is needed, and the strength of the lock on the gate.

That is, when our fear has a concrete, everyday object upon which to focus or fixate, we are on miserable yet dependably familiar ground, seemingly far from the quicksands of our deeper fears. Thus do we tend to prefer the burdened beasts of depression to the monsters of the deep.

And so thus do we tend to cling, however indirectly, to our everyday fearfulness, focusing on its mental content much more than the raw feeling itself. We then leave the nature of fear out of our inquiry, settling instead for explanations for why we are afraid. It's easy to use our reasoning powers to distance ourselves from our fearfulness, yet even from the loftiest and most seemingly safe neocortical towers we are not entirely out of the reach of our core fears.

Until we move toward our fear, we will be bound by it.

2. WORKING WITH FEAR

The key to working effectively with fear is to get *inside* it.

This means, among other things, that we need to have a clear knowledge of all the ways in which we've learned to get away from fear, so that when one of them shows up, we're capable of looking *at* it — rather than through its eyes — and, to whatever degree, saying no thanks.

Getting inside fear means getting past its periphery, getting past its defining thoughts, getting past its propagandizing sentinels, getting past our *problematic* orientation to fear. Entering the dragon's cave.

Once we are within fear, under its skin, with our attention scanning our surroundings like a miner's headlamp, we can begin acquainting ourselves with its basic features, particularly those sensations and beliefs that together make it into a something we label "fear." The closer we get to it, the better we can see it.

However, we need to learn not to get close too quickly, not to move so fast that we can't keep digesting and integrating what we're experiencing. If we're entering something as intense as terror, we have to step very carefully. Taking on too much only increases our fear of fear.

So slowly and carefully we go, feeling our way in, remaining as aware as possible of our breathing, feelings, sensations, and intentions, keeping some connection with the "outside world," letting our Ariadne's thread of remembrance have some slack, but not so much that we forget to keep in palpable contact with it. In touch.

Asking certain questions of ourselves as we proceed can be very helpful: "What sensations am I experiencing in my belly, my diaphragm, my throat, my upper back, my forehead, my hands? And how are these changing? What is their texture, tone, temperature, directionality, color, shape? And what kind of mental processes are going on as I do this? And to *whom* is all of this arising?"

That is, we deliberately cultivate some curiosity as we make our way toward and into the den — we are on guard, but we are not all that solidly armored. It is also advantageous to view the storyline presented by your fear as just that, a *story* — treat it as you would a dream that you're beginning to suspect is indeed a dream.

Sometimes it may be useful to personify fear — and not only ours! — as a scared child, a very upset child, a child who is aching for our touch, our care, our love. As much as that child, that self-conscious locus of frightened vulnerability, may initially shrink from us, it is only for as long as we forget or avoid our compassion.

When we remain outside our fear, we remain trapped within it.

When we, however, consciously get inside our fear, it's as if it turns inside out. Getting inside our fear with wakeful attention and compassion actually *expands* our fear beyond itself. Once the contractedness at the center of fear ceases to be fueled, fear unravels, dissipates, and terminates its occupancy of us.

In entering our fear, we end our fear of it.

Through attending closely, caringly, and carefully to the particulars of our fear, we *decentralize* it, so that its intentions and viewpoint can no longer govern us. When the light goes on in the grottos of dread, then fear is little more than our case of mistaken identity having a bad day.

When we touch our fear with real caring, it de-tenses, de-compresses, usually quite quickly becoming something other than fear, something unburdened by fear's agendas or headlines. Fear met with an open heart does not usually take long to dissolve.

The key is to actively and decisively *disidentify* with our fear.

Then all that's happening is a fluxing mix of phenomena that we typically label "fear," along with the awareness of it. Then our fearful thoughts and assumptions do not center us.

When we no longer feel as though we're constellated around our fear, then fear is no longer so fearful — it may still experientially resemble fear, but it doesn't have us so compellingly hooked. We may still be squirming, we might even still be frightened, but we *know* we're not really in as much trouble as our fear initially announced to us.

But sometimes fear can slam into us with such force, such shocking intensity, that we are left devastated. Rape, war, heavy accidents, a sudden loss of sanity. Huge, huge blows. Even so, it is still possible to approach such trauma-centered fear — at the right pace and very, very carefully, with skilled help — and defuse it. Doing so means not just working at a mental level, nor simply relying on medication, but rather adopting an integral approach, working in fitting depth with our physical, mental, emotional, spiritual, and social dimensions.

In working with fear, it is also important to take into account *collective* fear. Ever since we became capable of destroying ourselves through nuclear means, our fear-level has skyrocketed, along with our fear-distractions (depression and self-numbing ranking high on the list). We know in our marrow that we feel threatened — at least on a physical level — regardless of how "successful" our compensatory strategies might appear to be.

As long as our desire to continue distracting ourselves from our suffering is stronger, or permitted to be more central, than our longing to be *truly* free, we will continue to be occupied — or *colonized* — by both fear and its "remedies" (not the least of which are the spiritually ambitious dreams and immortality aspirations of our me-centeredness).

Going to the core of fear deepens love and relational intimacy. In fact, it's only through openly facing our fear that genuine fearlessness arises. In fear, we do not feel safe; but in ego-transcending love, we feel and are safe, being in intimate resonance with that which cannot be harmed or left.

Awareness doesn't mind fear.

Nor does love.

3. THE ANATOMY OF DOUBT

Doubt is an inner questioning infused with uncertainty and, more often than not, enough agitation to make it a relatively unpleasant state. In an everyday sense, doubt is what happens mentally when we find ourselves stranded in ambiguity's darker carrels, trying to think our way out, stuck in cognitive traffic jams that catch us in their treads and flatten us as much as they fragment us.

Typical doubt is not much more than skepticism that, having lost its clarity and confidence, is bound up in worrisome shades of uncertainty. Anxiety may be lurking nearby, ready to be recruited, bringing more of an edge to doubt. Although doubt is not dread, it can become dread if sufficiently fed.

Doubt can manifest as avoidance, moral impotence, indecisiveness, existential fence-sitting, indulgence in ambiguity, cognitive obsessing, prevarication, and so on — and it can also, though much less often, manifest as a necessary questioning, a courageous inquiry that can both tolerate and investigate uncertainty. Doubt is no more "bad" than "certainty" is good.

There's everyday doubt, a self-contracted, often neurotic questioning injected with constricted feeling, zigzagging with myopic desperation through the presenting layers of uncertainty; and there's another doubt, a sober questioning that carries us beyond facile certainties and automated beliefs deep into the inherent insecurity and uncertainty of Life, inviting us to adopt a *nonproblematic* orientation toward it.

Everyday doubt is a collapse of heart that has gone to mind, an unhappy, unillumined inquiry that's interested not in discovery or revelation, but only in persisting in repetitively touring its culs-de-sac. It puts an abundance of energy into going nowhere, spinning its wheels until it is exhausted, leaving us asleep at the wheel.

Such doubt is the contracted and divided mind doing time in uncertainty's mental mazes, providing apparent justification for worry.

Whereas skepticism is a healthy, incisive, and often robust questioning, everyday doubt is an unhealthy, indecisive, and chronically anaemic questioning, a dead-end inquiry, a bottled-up questioning that is terrified of being uncorked.

When the energy of everyday doubt is allowed to mushroom in our headquarters, it tends to invade and stain whatever content is nearby, immediately framing it in a darkly questionable light.

While immersed in doubt, we frequently inject fearfulness or negative anticipation into various intentions, plans, doings, and so on, obsessing about possible outcomes, chaining ourselves to chronic worry.

Doubt is what the mind tends to do both when it is cut off from the vitality and openness and primal intentions of our depths, and when rationality itself just does not satisfy. And doubt presumes to have an overview, but in fact has none — it cannot even see itself, let alone accurately assess its environment.

Nevertheless, doubt is *not* an enemy. What matters is what we do with it. Do we identify with it? Do we give our power away to it? Do we allow it to enlarge? Do we believe in it? Do we make decisions based on it? Or do we illuminate it, outbreathe and outdance it, crashing its slumber-party with such resolute focus that it cannot help but dissolve into a more Life-giving form?

Trying to work with doubt through mental means only doesn't really work. The self-suppression that catalyzes and animates doubt must be seen, felt, and known from the deep inside. Our whole being must be eased, expanded, given permission to come alive. Our torso must be loosened, our limbs unfrozen, our heart reentered, our reach made both powerful and vulnerable, so that our entire anatomy is brought into supportive resonance with what-really-matters.

Doubt must be seen for what it is without getting lost or absorbed in its point of view. Only then will it unfist itself; only then will our endarkened familiarity with it come unstrung; only then will our indecisiveness be unequivocally undone, flung into the raw reality of what we are, so that we might take our needed stands.

When doubt infects you, don't give it a thought. Neither avoid it nor let it recruit your mind.

Doubt your doubt, and then pour your undivided attention into whatever noncognitive openings have been generated by doing so.

When doubt does manage to infiltrate your mind, read its contents once-through as though they belonged to a supermarket tabloid, taking careful note of which headlines most easily snare your attention. Then immediately shift your attention, and shift it completely, to the feeling of your doubt, resisting the temptation to scoot back into your mind.

No matter how tempting it is to immerse yourself in what your doubt is telling you, shift your attention from whatever it is that you're doubting to the actual phenomenon of doubt itself. Feel into and through its tensions, its contracted tones, its positioning, its emotional qualities, its bodily ramifications and anatomical peculiarities; feel what it is doing to you, feel what it is doing to others near you, feel how it's staining your speech, vision, hearing, perception, posture, your very being...

And do this without trying to change or trash your doubt!

Sometimes simply keeping your attention on your doubt as an energetic phenomenon, as opposed to focusing on its content, will cause it to dissolve. Other times, deliberately doubting your doubt will make it dissipate.

Doubt may also sometimes be defused by taking a risk of being, such as a difficult but very much needed movement toward someone or a timely expressing of something painful that needs to be said, especially if these are done not in order to get rid of doubt, but because they are imperatives arising from something much deeper than our everyday mind and conditioning.

When the light goes on in the slums of doubt, then doubt is little more than skepticism having a bad day.

The key is to actively and decisively *disidentify* with our doubt, while also allowing the surfacing and fitting expression of whatever feeling states are associated with it — fear, sadness, anger, shame, and so on.

Do not make doubt wrong. Simply realize that when you lose yourself in doubt, you are shortcircuiting a deeper song.

When doubt infects you, don't mind it. Neither avoid it nor let it recruit your mind. Don't give it a thought. Instead, simply be aware of it.

Approach the infected areas with great care. No antibiotic heroics, no psychosurgical wizardry, just ordinary everyday caring.

Touch the infection with undivided attention, while letting the raw reality of it touch you, penetrate you, shake you more awake. Stop treating your doubt like an adversary or disease.

Don't give your doubt a thought. Instead, give it your full attention. Go right to its core. Its dark heart is but the shell, the calcified chambering, of a love that effortlessly dissolves all fear and clears space for a deeper life.

4. FEAR IN RELATIONAL STAGES

In me-centered relationships, fear mostly does as it pleases. Worry is usually taken to be normal. Anxiety often runs rampant. Fear and shame commonly hook up to generate guilt. Partners rarely share their fear. The "I" that is afraid is almost always left unexamined, except externally. Medication is strongly preferred over psychotherapy when it comes to dealing with fear.

There is great shame for men here in admitting that they are afraid. And when women do, their partners usually just want to fix them, and the more quickly, the better. Fear is almost always identified with, fled, disowned, marginalized, or camouflaged.

Here, we don't stand apart from fear in healthy detachment, but instead dissociate from it, deny its existence, or busy ourselves conquering some fears (like skydiving or public speaking) in order to avoid dealing with deeper fears. The very self (ego-centered and therefore over against the rest of existence) that centers this stage is itself inherently fearful (living as it does in a me versus not-me universe), so it is no surprise that fear is so rampant here.

In we-centered codependent relationships, fear generally is more openly admitted, but is still largely avoided. Worry usually still is taken to be normal, anxiety is common, and fear and shame continue to spawn guilt. The "I" that is afraid is largely supplanted by the "we" that is afraid, living as it does in a we versus them universe.

At this stage we may actually see the treasure — whereas the me-centered typically romanticize rather than see it — and really want it, but we're not about to face the dragons guarding it. Fear is lessened by avoiding highly stimulating circumstances. The price we pay for dulling our fear is high — a parallel dulling in the rest of our emotional life — but we go ahead anyway, in order to protect our cult of two from any serious tremors from within. Psychotherapy and medication are on equal footing here with regard to dealing with fear.

In we-centered coindependent relationships, fear is acknowledged and explored to some extent, but mostly only intellectually. Worry is not taken as normal, and anxiety is less common. Guilt only infrequently arises. The "we" that centers the relationship has enough connection to the larger or more collective "we" so as to not be so fear-based as in the previous stage.

Here we get a little closer to the dragons, but not close enough to really feel their heat. Fear is still dulled some, but is also approached, regardless of its bulk or fangs. The treasure is clearly in sight, just out of reach. Psychotherapy (especially in combination with meditation) is preferred here to medication when it comes to dealing with fear.

In being-centered relationships, we cultivate enough intimacy with the dragons to access the treasure they are guarding. That is, we get inside our fear, mining its depths for insight and keys to what lies beyond all fear. We don't dull our fear, so that it may at times appear to be stronger than in earlier stages. But whatever its strength, we are able to work with it.

At this stage, fear is not an enemy, but rather just unpleasant feeling energy-contraction. When it gets intense, it is allowed to sharpen our focus. We now have the ability to expand our energy, our core vitality, to such an extent that fear usually does not take long to mutate into excitement.

Through recognizing that fear can arise at any stage and through ceasing to identify with it, we stop making a problem out of its presence, using that very presence to enrich and deepen our lives.

This silken glide
This succulent ride
This ecstatic dying
This joy beyond trying
This melting mutuality
This everwild commonality
This rupturing rapture
This which no words can capture
This pleasure beyond pleasure
This depth none can measure
This the heartland of bliss
This the Holy Deep's naked kiss
This, this the art
  that cannot be framed
This, this the beauty
  that cannot be named
This, this the love
  that cannot be contained

IV. Sexuality

Chapter Twenty

EROS UNDRESSED: INTO THE HEART OF SEX

Sex is, not surprisingly, a highly charged topic when considering the anatomy and evolution of intimate relationship.

How-to books and courses on sex abound, pointing out various ways to get turned-on or more turned on in our relationship, with little or no attention given to actually exploring the very *turned-off-ness* that seemingly necessitates finding out how to get turned-on. Judging from the sheer volume of such books and courses, plus an immense amount of personal testimony from all quarters (for example, the *great* number of American women who admit that they don't enjoy sex with their husbands), it appears that there's an abundance of sexual dysfunction and dissatisfaction going on in relationships.

There is plenty of focus on this, accompanied by all kinds of remedies, but not nearly so much focus on how dysfunction and dissatisfaction in the *nonsexual* areas of relationship might be affecting our sexuality.

We are usually quite reluctant to cast (or even to permit the casting of) a clear light on what is *actually* happening during our sexual times with our partner — other than biologically — but without this, we are simply left in the dark, pinning too much on what we hope sex will do for us.

And there is *so* much that we expect sex to do for us! More often than we might like to admit, we assign it to stress-release, security-enhancement, spousal pacification, egoic gratification, pleasure-production, and other such tasks. We may use it as a super sleeping pill, a rapid-action pick-me-up, an agent of consolation, a haven or hideout, a control tactic, a proof that we're not that old or cold. We may also employ it as a psychological garbage disposal, a handy somatic terminal for discharging the energies of various unwanted states, like loneliness or rage or desperation — thereby turning our partner into little more than an outhouse for such feelings. Mostly, though, we just tend to want sex to make us feel better, and use it accordingly, whether in mundane, dark, or spiritual contexts.

Thus do we get screwed.

And to take the edge off being thus screwed, where do we primarily turn? To sex, and not necessarily just in the form of intercourse. So-called sexual addiction is, as we shall see, not really about sex, but about that for which sex is a "solution." It is so easy to think that our sexual charge with a particular situation is no more than an expression of our natural sexuality, when in fact it may actually just be an *eroticizing* of our conditioning or some need we have (for example, our arousal in a certain pornographic fantasy may only be *secondarily* sexual, its primary impetus being rooted in our longing to be unconditionally seen, loved, and wanted).

There won't, however, be any real freedom here until we release sex (and everything else) from the obligation to make us feel better.

So long as we keep assigning sex to such labor — slave labor — we will remain trapped in the very circumstances for which sexual release is an apparent "solution." Increased stress means an increased desire to get rid of stress, and if we attempt to do so through sexual means (which does not really get rid of stress, except in the most superficial sense), we simply reinforce the roots of our stress, as will be more thoroughly explained later. In addicting — or overattaching — ourselves to erotically pleasing release, we also frequently addict ourselves to the very tension that seemingly necessitates and sometimes even legitimizes such release.

The abuse of sex, particularly through the expectations with which we commonly burden it, is so culturally pervasive and deeply ingrained as to go largely unnoticed, except in its more lurid, obviously dysfunctional, or perverse extremes. Even more removed from any telling awareness is our aversion to truly exploring and illuminating the whole matter of human sexuality, not clinically, nor in any other kind of isolation (or in vitro corralling), but rather in the context of our entire being, our totality, our inherent wholeness.

That is, sex does not need to be — and in fact cannot be — crystallized out from the rest of our experience (as those overly focused on the mechanics of sexuality often try to do). Rather, it needs to be seen, felt, known, and lived in open-eyed resonance — and *relationship* — with everything that we do and are, so that it is, as much as possible, not just an act of specialized function, nor an act bound to the chore of making us feel better or more secure, but rather an unfettered, radiantly succulent, full-blooded expression of *already*-present, *already*-loving, *already*-unstressed wholeness.

To embody such wholeness requires a thorough investigation of the labor to which we have assigned — or *sentenced* — our sexuality.

That labor and its underpinnings are eloquently revealed through the stark slang of sex. Many of the words and phrases regarding our sexual functioning bluntly illustrate the frequently confused, disrespectful, and exploitive attitude commonly brought to our sexuality and sexuality in general. Consider, for example, the notorious and enormously popular "f" word, for which there are an incredible number of non-copulatory meanings, a fucking incredible number, all pointedly and colorfully describing what we may *actually* be up to when we are busy being sexual or erotically engaged.

Here's a partial list, the majority of which overlap in meaning with each other: ignorance ("Fucked if I know"); indifference ("I don't give a fuck"); degradation ("You stupid fuck"); aggression ("Don't fuck with me!"); disappointment ("This is really fucked"); rejection ("Get the fuck out of here!" or "Fuck off!"); manipulation ("You're fucking with my head"); disgust ("Go fuck yourself"); vexation ("What the fuck are you doing?"); exaggeration ("It was so fucking good!"); rage ("Fuck you!"); and, perhaps most pithily revealing of all, exploitation ("I got fucked").

Throw together the various meanings of "fuck," plus the "higher" or more socially acceptable terms for sexual intercourse — including the vague "having a relationship" and the unwittingly precise "sleeping together" — and mix in some insight, and what will emerge is a collage made up of (1) the dysfunctional labor to which we have sentenced our sexual capacity; and (2) the expectations (like "Make me feel wanted" or "Make me feel better") with which we have saddled and burdened it.

When we primarily assign our sexuality to stress-release, security-reinforcement, egoic reassurance, the fueling of romantic delusion, and other such chores — thereby just burdening it with the obligation to make us feel better — we are doing little more than screwing ourselves, dissipating much of the very energy that we need for facing and healing our woundedness, the woundedness that, ironically, we seek escape or relief from through the pleasuring and various sedating options provided by our sexuality.

This is not to say that we should never use our sexuality for purposes such as stress-release and egoic comfort — for there are times when doing so may be entirely appropriate — but that such usage needs to be more the exception than the rule.

We have, for at least the last 30 or 40 years, been living in a pervasively sexualized culture — "sexy" as an adjective has infiltrated just about every dimension of life — which is simultaneously underbounded and overbounded when it comes to sex. There's much more openness regarding sex than there was, say, 50 or 60 years ago, but much of that openness has more to do with *breadth* than depth.

We have more permission to experiment with sex and to talk graphically about it, but we nevertheless still don't talk about it in real depth very much, for to do so would put us in a position of real vulnerability, not so able to hang on to a semblance of "having it together."

And this is the era of informed consent, centered by the myth — yes, *myth* — of consenting adults. Many are, in sexual circumstances, not so much consenting adults as they are *adult*-erated children (and/or adolescents), whose consent — however "informed" — is very likely *not* coming from a clear consideration of what is going on and is at stake, but rather from a desire to get approval or more security.

Sex-as-sensation has come out of the closet — both in mundane and spiritual contexts — but not sex as radically intimate passion, needing no manuals or maps, conventional, tantric, and otherwise.

The deepest sex, sex requiring no fantasies (inner or outer) or turn-on strategies or rituals of arousal, but rather only the love, openness, and safety of awakened intimacy, cannot be significantly accessed without a corresponding depth in the *rest* of our relationship with our partner. Without such mutual maturity, it doesn't matter how hot or juicy or innovative our sexual life may be, even if we have many orgasms, big orgasms, together.

In fact, when we make coming together a goal, we simply come apart, separating and losing ourselves in our quest for maximally pleasurable sensations. "Sensational" sex is precisely that, sex that is centered and defined by an abundance of erotically engorged *sensations*. The romanticized presence of these sensations is often misrepresented as actual intimacy, at least until the rude pricks of reality do their vastly underappreciated job.

Most couples I see are not really all that happy with their sex life. Some have gone flat, having had little or no sex for a long time (not surprisingly, the rest of their relationship is also usually flat, low in passion, unnaturally peaceful). Others are more openly frustrated, wanting more than they are getting (such a quantitative bias being mostly a male complaint), or wanting more connection before sex (such a qualitative bias being mostly a female complaint). Others act as if they are doing fine sexually, not wanting, at least initially, to reveal their discomfort with the direction that their sex life may be taking (like tolerating a partner who prefers porn to them). And so on. The good news is that such dissatisfaction, *if* allowed to surface in its fullness, will often goad a couple into doing work that they would otherwise avoid or postpone (thereby serving their transition from me-centered to we-centered to being-centered).

As a couple explores their sexuality, and explores it deeply, they will discover that what's not working in their relationship usually shows up, often in exaggerated form, in their sexuality. And conversely, as they ripen into more mature ways of relating, they will find that this revitalizes and deepens their sexuality. No sex manuals are needed, nor any fantasies or other turn-on tactics — their increased intimacy and trust in each other is more than sufficient, creating an atmosphere within which love-centered, awareness-infused lust can naturally arise and flow, carrying the lovers along into the sweet dynamite and ever-fresh wonder and ecstasy of what sex can be when it has deep intimacy's green light.

To more fully explore sex in the context of intimate relationship, more background is needed. Hence the upcoming chapters on eroticism, pornography, the creation of charge, the eroticizing of our needs and conditioning, and flirting. Further chapters will explore sexuality in me-centered, we-centered, and being-centered relationships.

Deep sex does not promise happiness, but *begins* with happiness.

Chapter Twenty One

AN INSIDE LOOK AT EROTICISM

When the erotic becomes neurotic, eroticism arises — defined here as obsessive interest in sexual activity, opportunity, and possibility.

Just about everything that catalyzes or promises sexual stimulation and satisfaction is but an object for eroticism's calculating eye, something to buy shares in, something to package and profitably replicate, something to exploit.

Eroticism makes an idol out of sexual excitation, thereby bringing about an exaggerated attachment to whatever maximizes — or at least once maximized — such excitation. This intensifies not only our distress, but also our urge for release, especially the release that is provided by orgasm.

However, this release, whatever its marketing hype, is neither ecstasy nor liberation, but rather only *brief relief*, akin to the sensation felt when an extremely tight pair of shoes is at last removed. Repeatedly putting the shoes back on in order to later have — no, *necessitate* — a pleasurable release is fundamental to eroticism.

Understandably, eroticism is a popular refuge, given its power to divert our attention from our suffering. Among its attractions is its capacity to apparently discharge tension (what is usually not recognized here is that what's being discharged is not distress itself, but rather only the outer edges or *branchings* of distress).

Eroticism keeps us in heat, neurotically available for sexual activity, just as tightly bound to sexual possibility as anxiety is to threatening possibility.

With our not-so-difficult-to-buy cooperation, eroticism keeps our sex center open for business, not only as an entertainment complex bulging with steamy distraction and dreamy drama, but also as a psychological tension-dump or soporific.

Eroticism is kept on the burner by our very urge for release from its contractedness and underlying pain. Over and over again, we seek release from our craving to have sex *through* having sex, emptying ourselves of our eroticized craving even as we strengthen and complicate its roots, ever looking for a better pair of tight shoes.

That is, we crave getting rid of the intensity of sexual desire itself, feeling ourselves unable to tolerate its fleshed-out presence, even as we force-feed it again and again, eroticizing ourselves into a position where we just have to have some sort of release, some sort of orgasmic payoff, some kind of semi-blissful sedation, which only deprives us of the very energy that we need in order to truly investigate the source of our distress.

Eroticism promises happiness, but real sex *begins* with happiness.

Real sex is intimate play, spontaneous and fully alive, needing no distress for its intensity, no preconceived or mechanical stimulation for its passion, no fantasy for its ecstasy, no strategy for its depth.

Although sex in being-centered relationship includes intense stimulation at times, this is created not through strategic or merely frictional means, but instead spontaneously arises as a *natural byproduct* of the couple's love-play. They *already* feel good; they are not expecting sex to make them feel good. They are not suppressing their being and making a goal or grail out of release, for they are already released, already at ease, already in embrace with the heart of their desire, already present in lovingly erotic mutuality, already consciously and willingly consumed by their passion's fire and light.

By reinforcing and overselling the must in lust, eroticism just cheapens sexual desire, stripping it of much of its natural spontaneity and expansiveness, injecting it with compensatory fantasy. As such, eroticism is not much more than a misuse of imagination.

If we need to fantasize in order to have "good" sex, then we are not truly interested in sex, but rather only in a mind-game whose purpose is to maximize pleasurable sensation and release.

Sex does not require the thinking and image-generating activities of mind in order to function, and in fact will not flow fully and freely if thoughts and fantasies are allowed to intrude into and dominate its domain.

Probably the only useful function of the mind during sex is that of supporting psychic communion between lovers; the expansiveness and openness of mind implicit in this exists in stark contrast to eroticism, which is but a contraction of mind, a neon theater of dark dramatics, crawling with pornographic abstraction.

But what happens to eroticism when sex is no longer allowed to go to mind (or come from mind)? What becomes of eroticism when ecstasy is not the goal, but the *foundation*? What becomes of eroticism when love is already present, and both lovers are already open, relaxed, happy, and in deep communion?

Eroticism then simply transcends itself, becoming the playful expression of sexual desire and passion, its face that of longing, not a tense or ambitious longing, but a blissful, open-eyed longing, an achingly sweet longing to share our depths with our partner through sexplay that is as loving as it is lusty, as subtle as it is succulent, as wild as it is tender, as free from preconceived notions as it full of ever-fresh wonder.

The point is not to squash eroticism, but to illuminate it, to free it from its desperation and egoic agendas and mechanicalness, so that it might *outgrow* itself, becoming but available energy, cutting new, life-giving channels, ever deepening our embrace with our beloved.

Chapter Twenty Two

AN INSIDE LOOK AT PORNOGRAPHY

Pornography — sexually explicit material designed to catalyze and intensify sexual charge in loveless, aesthetically barren, and frequently degrading contexts — is basically just dehumanization in erotic drag, both depending upon and reinforcing obsessive interest in sexual activity and possibility. Pornography is the business of eroticism.

Pornography exploits the craving of those driven to distract themselves from their suffering through erotic excitation and discharge.

Pornography's pictures tell a story with usually the scantiest of plots, a story that brings together viewed and viewer in a quickly undressed hotbed of unillumined lust. Whether or not there's actual sex, everyone gets screwed.

Whatever helps to amplify sexual excitation is brought into the picture or plot; sometimes this is relatively innocuous, and other times it is darker, uglier, nastier, blurring the line between sexuality and violence. Pornography gives lust a bad name.

Pornography doesn't give a damn about whom it screws with, so long as it has their business.

Pornography is erotic imagination gone slumming, losing contact with love and ecstasy along the way.

And pornography is not just limited to dying-to-be-fucked centerfolds, "adult" movies, lurid romance novels, and so on, but is the primary operational strategy of those driven to employ fantasy in their sex life, especially as a means of getting turned on or staying aroused.

In binding our sexuality to our minds, overvaluing erotic stimulation, and reducing our partner to little more than a prop in our masturbatory drama, we don't see that we are only screwing ourselves. To truly enjoy sex is then out of reach for us, for we do not enter its domain nakedly present and loving, but come in already overly attached to erotic expectations and rituals which originally arose as "solutions" to our suffering.

Chronically distressed teenage boys who have discovered the pleasure and relief that ejaculation can provide likely will also find and employ various visuals, both externally (like magazine porn) and internally ("hot" girls at their school), that amplify their arousal. If fantasy-centered erotic arousal and discharge remains their method for reducing their distress as they leave their teens, and if they do not question nor attempt to dismantle such conditioning (as can be done through skillful therapy and/or awakening practices), they will likely retain it through their adult years, even in a loving relationship. They may keep it in the dark, but when it comes to crunch time — as when they want to feel *really* turned on — they will animate it, perhaps through sexually fantasizing while engaging in sex, or perhaps through viewing porn.

For pornography to cease being our erotic default, we need to reenter, become intimate with, heal, and integrate the *wounding* that originally drove — and still drives — us into pornography's domain. In doing so, we liberate our libido from its dark, loveless ruts.

In seducing ourselves with erotic tension and its mounting expectations, thereby building enough sexual excitation to necessitate— and perhaps even legitimize — some kind of release, we are already doing business with pornography.

Like any other business, pornography arises to meet consumer needs, and also does what it can to stimulate those needs. Horny capitalism. The advertising industry milks pornographic angles as much as it can, because it is good for business, especially in the hypersexualized setting of contemporary Western culture. If the worst of porn could amp up car sales, we'd probably glimpse some of it, however subtly incorporated, hanging around the shadier outskirts of car ads. This, of course, brings up questions of morality and the inevitable claiming of the high ground by religious zealots at one end of the pornographic spectrum, and by stay-out-of-my-sex-life apologists for porn at the other end.

But neither condemnation nor neurotic tolerance bring us any closer to dealing sanely with pornography. It still burns, and will burn, and burn far and wide, until we *stop sexualizing our distress* — which means releasing sex from the obligation to make us feel better.

Pornography's fire does not purify, but only inflames and engorges, both distracting us from our pain and bloating us with such heated urge that we seemingly have to have some sort of relief, or discharge of energy. However, such discharge doesn't rejuvenate or truly ease us, but instead only sedates us, dulling our edge and leaving us less motivated than ever to getting to the heart of what is driving us to so desperately seek the excitement and payoffs of our pornographic proclivities.

Pornography is far more pervasive than we might like to think. For example, conventional or typical romance is also arguably pornographic, however much it might appear otherwise. When fantasy-centered sexual anticipation or excitation gets an emotional grip on us, and when we mistake fusion with communion, such romance occurs. It is not much more than a chestful of lust packed with swooning idealism, deliciously stimulating imagery, and runaway hope, a hope hopelessly enthused about union, true love, and soulmate possibilities (all of which do, of course, occur in *mature* relationships), a hope nourished and sustained by the dissolution of boundaries. A sweetly narcotic spell of dramatic delusion...

In conventional or typical romance — the separative swoon of false oneness — boundaries are not expanded, so as to include the other, but are collapsed, abandoned, forgotten.

Eventually, as the passion loses some intensity and doubts creep in and the dream's fabric thins, the lovers start wondering where they went wrong, not seeing that what isn't working in the relationship has been there *all along*, obscured by the heat of their embrace and the giddy intensity of their fusion. They were but getting it on under artificial light, blindly merging where sensation and idealism meet, abandoning their boundaries instead of stretching them.

Nevertheless, even though many of us do recognize the folly of such romance, we still tend to support it, acting as if it's still a lovely thing, an essential part of love, when in fact it is not love at all, but only an intoxicating cocktail of idealism, hope, and perfumed pornography, marketing a pleasurably consoling dream in which sentimentalized eroticism is mistaken for love, and undiscerning certainty for truth.

And how do we know when we're in the grip of conventional romance? We feel swoony, off balance, intoxicated, marooned from our critical faculties, unquestioningly immersed in our cosy cult of two, our little bubble of immunity, happily unaware of the rude pricks of reality that our very situation is attracting. It is a delicious dream, happily feverish and often laced with mystical elements (like boundary dissolution and blissfulness), and therefore not so easy to wake up from, but wake up from it we must, if we are to find and live in real love, the kind of love that makes possible a sexuality that is ecstatically present.

Pornography is a perversion or dark detouring of our longing to openly and fully express our true sexual capacity, to come alive with sensual and sexual delight, to totally embrace and celebrate our erotic potential.

Pornography is but a calculating child locked in a forgotten room, too lonely to weep, marooned from innocence, compulsively taking the edge off its distress through self-pleasuring erotic rituals, again and again seeking the perfect replication of its most satisfying releases, surrounding itself with whatever does the best job.

There's no point in preaching about how terrible pornography is, and nor is there any point in getting liberal or righteously tolerant about it. Merely permitting pornography to speak and exhibit itself, out of some twisted notion of human rights, does no one any good.

Yes, pornography's voice must be heard, but not passively! It must be given room to extend itself beyond itself, until its roots are exposed. Allowing this is not the action of the weak or supposedly tolerant, but rather the action of those who know their own pornographic inclinations so intimately that they are no longer under their spell.

Instead of just repressing or indulging in our pornographic leanings, we'd do better by exploring them and journeying to the heart of the pain and disconnection underlying them. Instead of guilting ourselves for having a pull toward pornography, we can gaze both at it and at our attraction to it with resolute compassion on our way to its underlying pain, finding the courage to ask for skilled guidance in this if necessary.

Pornography will not cease until we recognize — and recognize more than just intellectually — how we create our distress, compassionately turn toward it, and do whatever is necessary to bring about the needed healing. Until then we will crave release from the distress we bring to ourselves, and will repeatedly betray ourselves in both the indulgence and the repression of our desire for such release, drowning our integrity in misguided notions of right and wrong, notions that arise not from our being, but from our conditioning.

Enter sexuality's domain when you are already happy, already unstressed, already loving, and you will not need to invite in your mind and its pornographic offerings, nor turn the lights out.

Chapter Twenty Three

THE EROTICIZING OF OUR NEEDS

To eroticize our needs means to both (1) sexually frame them and (2) seek their fulfillment (or at least something resembling their fulfillment) through sexual activity.

Much of sexuality is not much more than such eroticizing. Some men, for example, may think that they are very sexual — wanting to have sex several times every day with their partner — when in fact they are not really very sexual, but rather are simply overloaded with anger, so much so that they find (however unknowingly) considerable energetic release of that anger through their sexuality. They have just eroticized their need to release their anger.

Another example: Some women may act very sexual — making a show of being in almost nonstop heat — when in reality they are simply very insecure, and have found increased security, material and otherwise, through presenting themselves as overly available sexually. They have just eroticized their need for security.

We can eroticize just about anything, plugging our original excitation (whether positive *or* negative) regarding it into sexual channels, thereby simultaneously reliving it — however indirectly — *and* finding some release from it. If we, for example, were severely neglected during our childhood, we may have a "charge" with current situations which feature some kind of neglect (because we are drawn, however mechanically, to whatever mimics that which is unresolved in us).

In considering our erotically-harnessed "solutions" for dealing with past difficulties — low self-esteem, family problems, anxiety, and so on — the explicitly sexual details are not so important as the setting, context, and dramatic particulars. Our sexual arousal might, for example, have much to do with simply wanting to be nonjudgmentally noticed by an obviously attentive fantasy partner. Yes, our excitation regarding this may manifest sexually in our fantasy, but it is only *secondarily* sexual, its primary impetus being rooted in a longing to be openly loved and seen.

This can be further fleshed out and given deserving depth by closely examining the supporting props (clothing, furniture, words spoken, and so on) in our fantasy — for such details say much about the original context out of which our fantasy arose, perhaps making possible a reconstruction of previously unintegrated events. (For example, a man who as a boy was neglected by his mother may as an adult redirect his negative excitation regarding this into sexual fantasies that feature him receiving unquestioningly open and easy sexual attentiveness from women who, before disrobing before him, are wearing the same colors that his mother often did.)

Consider a darker example: A man frequents sadomasochistic parlors, getting the most sexual pleasure out of being whipped. In his fantasies he associates sexuality with violence, and is drawn to porn that features this association. Some might think he's just sexually kinky (and also perhaps that what he's doing is fine, so long as it's between "consenting" adults), but what's truer is that he's deeply wounded.

Take away the erotic overlay in his fantasies and practices, and what's left is violence and a gaping lack of love. It's no big surprise to find out he was severely beaten almost daily, literally whipped bloody, by his mother during his boyhood, and that that was the only touch he got from her.

Eroticizing his internalized and undealt-with violence simply took the edge off it, providing a way to discharge the surfacing pain of it; but stripping it down to its roots made possible a healing that quickly eroded his interest in sadomasochistic porn and practices. Once the original pain had been openly felt and skillfully worked with, there was no longer any need to sexualize it.

And another example: A woman, clearly heterosexual, finds to her embarrassment that the most erotically vital fantasies for her involve other women. No men are present. She's had some sexual encounters with other women, but these just didn't work for her. What's going on in her fantasies is a women-only encounter; but take away the erotic dimension, and all that is actually occurring is women being closely connected to each other.

This woman grew up in a home with a violent father and brothers, and found her only comfort, however minimal, in the company of her mother and aunts. Quite understandably, she has a considerable charge with being in a setting which features the safety and warmth of other women, a setting in which she can really relax and let go. The fact that she has eroticized this simply means that it represents something that has generated excitation in her for a long time.

(Another cause of a heterosexual woman having sexual fantasies about other women may simply be that the women she fantasizes about have the kind of body she wishes that she had, and that if they find her attractive — as demonstrated by wanting to be sexual with her — then she must be as sexy and attractive as they are. She thus owns that fantasy body, if only for a moment.)

So our erotic fantasies are tales well worth investigating, tales that reveal much about us. What they dramatize is simply the eroticizing — arising from the excitement, however negative — of our longing to be fulfilled, safe, loved, needed, seen, touched, and known, and perhaps also our longing to find release from past difficulties and trauma through the very excitation (however unpleasant or terrifying) catalyzed by such difficulties and trauma. The intensity of the pleasure or release that they promise is a marker of the intensity of the pain which we are trying to bypass.

Some erotic fantasies may be quite complex, but their themes are not; in fact, such complexity might just reflect a need to have many things in order or under control so that the desired outcome can occur, a need that likely has its roots in many things having been out of order or control in our early years. But whatever their detailing, our eroticized needs are just that — needs. Strip them of their erotic overlay and presentation, and what remains is what is not yet healed.

Once we realize that the eroticizing of our needs and unresolved wounds is both an escape from suffering *and* a mark of it, we put ourselves in a position where we can free our sexuality from the obligation to make us feel better.

The charge we have with what is unresolved in us is simply that, an excitation (whether positive or negative) or energetic intensity rooted in our reaction to various events from our past; when we reroute this excitation into the pleasuring possibilities of sex, we are literally moving away from the pain that underlies such excitation, the pain that, when consciously entered and illuminated, can liberate us.

To de-eroticize our needs and wounds is to see them in their rawness, and to turn toward what we *really* need.

Chapter Twenty Four

TAKING CHARGE OF OUR CHARGE

Sexual excitation — the *amplification* of which will be referred to from now on as *charge* — is not just something that happens to us, but often is also something that we, however unknowingly, generate in ourselves.

We are in charge of our charge, however strongly we might be inclined to think of ourselves otherwise. It is natural to feel sexually attracted to certain people at certain times, but not so natural to translate and amplify that attraction — or psychogravitational pull — into charge.

The transition from attraction to charge is an unknown territory to many of us, a largely dehumanized zone overpopulated by the conviction that the seductive promises lining its hormonal highways are there of their own accord, independent of us. This leaves us in the position of innocent bystander or victim, conveniently separate from — and far from responsible for! — the erotic heating-up we are experiencing.

So what is charge? It is fundamentally just biochemical thrill on the make, mixing together amplified sensation and erotic anticipation. A cocktail of sweet dynamite. Regardless of its outfitting and presentation, charge mostly is just the leading edge — or wedge — of unilluminated lust.

Most of all, however, it is something that *we* are doing to ourselves, something erotically engrossing and excitingly compelling, something we engage in not so as to awaken from our conditioning, but rather so as to exploit its possibilities. Making out in prison makes it seem less like prison — at least until charge wanes, and we once again busy ourselves rebuilding and restaging it, looking to its engorged meatiness and hotly enveloping dramatics for enough warmth to keep the chill realization of what we are *really* up to at bay.

The creation of charge, and especially the repetitive creation of charge, mostly is no more than compensation for the apparent loss of — or, more accurately, estrangement from — what we naturally are. In short, a pleasurably consoling refuge from what troubles us. Something that quickly makes us feel better, efficiently distracting us from what we would rather not face.

The craving to create charge, to suffuse (and perhaps even overwhelm) ourselves with its sweetly surging sensations, is mostly just a confession of being marooned from our depths. A booby prize in the making. Beneath its pinkened periphery and hormonal heights, charge actually is quite desperate, overly concerned with both its satisfaction and its continuation.

But just what gets satisfied? Not us.

Sex cannot truly satisfy and nourish us if charge persists as its foundation and central characteristic. In fact, sex can then only degenerate, until the distance or numbness or turned-off-ness that was there all along is at last undeniably present, daylight naked, soaking up attention and energy (thereby leaving lovers wondering where their original passion went).

Real sex does not depend upon charge. Its passion arises not so much from stimulation, as from an intimacy rooted in deep mutual trust, an intimacy that relies on the most potent of all aphrodisiacs: wide-awake, unconditioned love, soul-anchored love, love in the raw, love that is but the feeling of edgeless, already-sentient openness, communion, and connection.

As it is usually employed, charge is little more than erotic self-advertising, serving to proclaim our sexual readiness, availability, and potency. When we are thus possessed by charge — overvaluing it to the point where we are unresistingly seeing through its eyes — just about everything around us with any sexual valence tends to be considered as a potential object for its appetite, a possible harbinger of erotic possibility, to be classified as fuckable, unfuckable, or worth checking out.

Nevertheless, charge can be a very positive thing, as when it arises between partners living together in genuine intimacy. Then charge becomes but a succulent rush and richly thrilling swell that supports and celebrates our intimacy.

When we, however, create charge with someone other than our partner (as is especially common in me-centered relationships), we usually then only create (or reinforce) distance between ourselves and our partner, all but ensuring that our intimacy with him or her won't go any deeper. Which may be what "we" actually want.

Flirting — teasing spiked with sexual innuendo — with those other than our partner keeps us "safely" in the shallows, regardless of the depths suggested by our bedroom eyes and body language (for more on flirting, see the next chapter). Animating and indulging our promiscuous capacity, however subtly or discretely, keeps our intimacy with our partner unnecessarily unstable, for we, through the irresponsibly eroticized wandering of our attention, are then betraying — or are at least dangerously close to betraying — our relationship with our partner.

And thus do we "protect" ourselves from reaching the point with our partner where we have gone too far to have an exit from intimacy's demands, instead distracting and immunizing ourselves with neurotic suggestiveness and its titillating payoffs.

The point, however, is not to repress charge, but rather to become as conscious as possible of our relationship to it, so that we might cease needing to advertise our sexual availability, and cease being slaves to the creation and imperatives of charge, and cease relying on the presence of charge to make us feel better.

When we move beyond teasing ourselves and others with the promises and possibilities of eroticism, we are in a position to embody a deeper pleasure, a pleasure that eventually transmutes into ecstasy. Then we can feel the presence of the Truly Significant, letting that feeling permeate, light up, and magnify our bond with our partner.

When we let our charge be in charge, when we overassociate sexuality with sensation, God then is reduced to the Ultimate Orgasm. When we hobble charge with guilt, God is reduced to the Ultimate Peeping Tom.

At the same time, however, squashing charge keeps us busy playing vigilant zookeeper or leak-inspector, trying to ensure that our erotic heatedness remains properly or nicely contained. Eviscerating charge simply desiccates us, creating in us an exaggerated (or even pathological) interest in religious, philosophical, or political watering holes.

The fantasies we erect and inhabit through the engineering of charge do not necessarily need a wrecking ball, nor quarantine, nor moral righteousness, nor more fire exits, but rather only sufficient compassion to touch the loneliness, fear, and pain that crouch in their shadows. When we undress charge and give it enough heart, it becomes but liberated energy, revealing what we're all dying to see and feel.

Taking charge of our charge involves a no that makes possible a deeper yes. And in that yes exists a joy that is our birthright, welcoming all that we are.

Chapter Twenty Five

THE ANATOMY OF FLIRTING

To flirt is to show casual, superficial, or apparently superficial interest in someone or something (as in flirting with an idea or a project), but for the purposes of this chapter it will be primarily defined as a subset of the above: Teasing which is spiked, however subtly, with sexual innuendo, interest, or invitation. Much is suggested or implied, and little is directly stated, for directness usually deflates the dance of flirtatiousness, robbing it of much of its ceremony and color.

To explore flirting is to explore personal and interpersonal boundaries. Flirting, like any other sexually-flavored undertaking, tends to magnify whatever dynamics are already present, and so is especially revealing regarding the operational status of the boundaries of those caught up in flirtatious connection. That is, flirting highlights our relationship (or *lack* of relationship) with our boundaries — *if* we will take a step back from it, so as to bring it more into focus.

In me-centered relationships, flirting is about as commonplace as the rationalizations for it. Those who complain about their partner's flirtatious behavior with others often have their complaints dismissed as mere possessiveness, oversensitivity, or just plain delusion. "I was just joking around" and "I wasn't doing anything wrong" are just two of many possible rejoinders proclaiming the flirter's innocence.

Other reactions — like "You've got nothing to worry about" or "Haven't you got better things to do?" — conveniently turn the focus back on the complaining or concerned other. Deflection, denial, avoidance, and so on — such strategies allow the flirter to bypass taking an inside look at what's *really* going on.

The presentation of a clean exterior and an innocent interior is a strategy to keep one's egoity intact. Those who are thicker may claim no fault whatsoever — these are the ones who *won't* say that they are sorry — but those who are a bit more clever will trot out statements like "I'm just human" or "Nobody's perfect" or "I'm doing my best" (which may be the most widely used and widely accepted of all excuses for bad behavior).

And it can get ugly: Sometimes the one doing the flirting may tell their partner that they're crazy to think that there's anything to worry about, and not stop implanting this notion even when the flirting leads to an affair. Partners at this stage mostly don't and won't listen to each other when they get the message that there are things that they ought not to be doing. When sexual possibilities, however fleeting or hands-off, arise, the betrayal of our partner — whether it's acted-out or not — is common, with integrity either being nonexistent or just a distant, impotent echo from our moral outback.

Even when there is no clearly overt flirting, the very fact that its presence, regardless of its level of dormancy, exerts such a strong pull keeps relationships at this stage unstable. Depth and true connection come in far behind the promises and opportunities of being sexually pleasured, however indirectly. Ironically, this is also the relational stage where romanticism (the illusion of true connection and depth) is strongest. Those here expect a great relationship without doing anything significant to bring that about. It's all about satisfying me, taking care of me, feeding me. Monogamy here is not much more than romanticism, security-craving, and sloppy boundaries striking a deal.

Since marriage in general signals a loss of freedom for men at this stage, flirting for them wields considerable appeal, because it *seems* to expand

and open them, through widening their field of possibilities; they have simply eroticized their craving not to be confined. And for women here, marriage mostly means an increase in security, with the result that flirting for them is often an attractive option, because it seems to increase or reinforce their sense of power, especially through being able to magnetize men's attention — which helps to strengthen their sense of security. So at this stage flirting for men offers a kind of pseudo-liberation, a break from the hemming-in they ordinarily associate with marriage or committed relationship; and for women it offers a kind of pseudo-empowerment, a furthering of the sense of security that can come from being desired.

In we-centered codependent relationships, flirting is far less of an issue, usually not drawing much energy from either partner, especially the woman. Flirting here doesn't disappear, but simply goes underground. Nevertheless both partners sense, however subtly, both its presence and what its presence signals. They have a tacit agreement not to directly address it, even as they judge other couples whom they see flirting.

In their minds they are, however, frequently still acting out sexually with others. If they remember having dreams of doing so, they are unlikely to share them with their partner. If they stay together for more than a few years, their libido tends to drop so low that the possibility of flirting loses almost all of its appeal, along with potential affairs; and this creates the illusion of a deeper security and peace with each other than is actually the case.

But it's a false peace, an all-but-dead peace, haunted by cries from deep within. If these cries are not heeded, the body starts to act up, rebel, make a fuss: All kinds of hard-to-explain symptoms show up, conveying the message that something important is not being heard.

In avoiding flirting, and therefore also the betrayal inherent in flirting, we-centered codependent couples avoid having to deal with it and its roots, thereby betraying themselves, staying away not only from exterior threat — flirtatious behavior — but also from interior threat — the calling for more depth and the risks which make that possible. Stuck in-between, the couple slowly stagnates, attempting to homestead in a relational flatland.

In we-centered coindependent relationships, things are generally much the same, except that flirting is less submerged. It sometimes may even be made allowable for both partners, as a demonstration of "respecting" each other's autonomy. If flirting is threatening to one member of the couple, the other usually listens, and changes his or her behavior. Flirting here is mostly seen for what it is, including its underlying motivation and agendas, but nevertheless still remains significantly rooted.

In being-centered relationships, flirting simply disappears, except with our partner, where it takes shape mostly as a loving playfulness infused with some degree of sexual energy. And why does flirting thus disappear at this stage? Because our urge for it (other than toward our partner) has no energy behind it.

This is *not* repression. There is no desire to seek — or to titillate ourselves with the possibility of — intimate sexual fulfillment with anyone other than our partner. Whatever might distract us from our intimacy with our partner simply carries no appeal for us.

At this stage we have not condemned flirting, nor ostracized it, nor sentenced it to some internal dungeon, but have simply *outgrown* it. If we do anything that resembles flirting, it is only with each other. Just as we may lose the taste for a certain food, we have lost the taste for flirting, but, unlike those in we-centered bonds, have not lost or diluted our deep passion for each other.

In fact, by not having — and not needing — any distractions from our connectedness with each other, we find an ever-deepening passion for each other, which grows in parallel with the deep intimacy we so knowingly and gratefully share. Our attention for each other does not wander, nor is forced, but is utterly natural. We have not so much chosen such relationship, but have reached a point where there is really nothing else for us to do in the realm of relationship.

If we are in a committed intimate relationship, flirting with anyone other than our partner is just eroticized neurosis. It is at best morally adolescent. Even if we actually are not advertising our sexual availability through our flirtatiousness, we are still nonetheless titillating ourselves, amping up our arousal levels, without really taking a telling look at our apparent need to do so. (The craving to get turned on is mostly just a confession of being *turned off*. We'd do much better to explore, deeply explore, that turned-off-ness, rather than camouflage it with our efforting to get turned on.)

Flirting with anyone other than our partner is not just eroticism on the make (sometimes showing up as the "nicer" side of pornography), but also a betrayal of our partner. It doesn't matter how subtle or removed it is, or whether or not our partner even notices — it is still a betrayal, an irresponsible wandering of attention, a making of sexual charge with another more important than our bond with our partner. Not to thus wander is not repression, but rather a life-giving choice, an act of integrity, a no that makes possible a deeper yes, a turning away that deepens our turning toward what matters most of all.

And if we were to strip flirting of its erotic components, its horny hoping and dressed-up groping and arousing jousting, what do we have left, besides playfulness and proximity? A riveting, eye-to-eye attentiveness from another. Energized focus from another. We then are the center of another's attention.

If we have any charge, positive or negative, with being the center of others' attention — a souvenir (or hangover) from childhood — then we are going to be drawn to situations in which we are, or can be, the center of others' attention, and as adults we are likely going to *eroticize* such a charge, just because it makes the whole thing a lot more appealing, while conveniently obscuring the underlying dynamics. (The tendency to eroticize our unresolved issues, issues with which we still have a charge, be it positive or negative, was discussed in the previous chapter.)

The cessation of flirting with anyone other than our partner does not, however, necessarily mean the cessation of playfulness and teasing (although in we-centered relationships the repression of flirting tends to suppress playfulness and teasing, simply because energy itself is being suppressed). Teasing, in fact, is an important ingredient in the relational mix, allowing much to be shared that otherwise would be left unshared, only superficially shared, or shared with considerable difficulty.

Let's now conclude by looking at flirting within a committed intimate relationship. Such flirting, even though it is only with our partner, is not always healthy, often being just a mechanically suggestive ritual advertising our erotic interest in our partner (or in what our partner can do for us), a self-stimulating presentation of our potential availability for some sort of sexual encounter, often with little real concern for connection with our partner.

However, when openness, attunement, and loving mutuality are already the case, so that the dramatics of such flirting constitute not an avoidance or simulation of such qualities, but rather a wakeful, passionately loving play upon them, then we are in the realm of *healthy flirting*, which there is no need to cut through, any more than there is to remove the feathers from a mating peacock, or to halt the beautifully ragged flight of coupling butterflies.

Such flirting's theatricalness is both heartfelt and mischievous, heated and luminous, dynamic and subtle, generously punctuated by a humor that spontaneously includes within itself a refreshingly open overview of the flirting itself — all of which only deepens our relationship.

Unhealthy flirting within a committed intimate relationship signals a separation of heart and sexuality, of love and desire, of sensation and feeling, reinforcing the must in lust. It's not only a fire that's all heat and no light, however bright its gaze, but also a strategy for distracting ourselves from our pain and uncertainty, through generating and getting behind the wheel of a mood of erotic possibility. In this context, sex with our partner is simply reduced to the task of making us feel better.

Such flirting is but diseased foreplay, rubbing us the wrong way, setting up a friction that seemingly necessitates — and perhaps also appears to justify — some kind of release. There's no real joy in this, but only lewdly winking or coyly shrinking desperation, only seductively smiling manipulativeness, only a clinging to pleasure-possibilities that maroons us from real joy and connection with our partner.

Healthy flirting within a committed intimate relationship is an unrehearsed drama of love and lust, of heat and light, of rough and tender, of give and take, an improvised dance of grace and fire, of thrust and bend, of erotic care and communion. It is intimacy taking the dancefloor, dressed for the part, stripped of solemnity and shoulds, unburdened by nostalgia (for both past and future) and romantic delusion.

Such flirting is but the face of playful desire, already happy, already loose, juicy and relaxed, turned on but not turned tight, beaming bright, inviting us to dance with our partner until we are both being danced, spun, undone, left radically alive in awakened intimacy's crucible, freed through the depth and intensity of our commitment to going all the way together.

Chapter Twenty Six

SEX IN THE STAGES OF INTIMATE RELATIONSHIP

In me-centered relationships, sex is not much more than a matter of making ends meet.

Arousal has exaggerated importance here, as does gratification. Whatever amplifies pleasurable sensation is, most of the time, unquestioningly taken to be a good thing. The eroticizing of our needs and wounds is as commonplace as it is unnoticed. Whatever its intensity may be at this stage, sex generally is just all heat and no light, harnessed more often than not to pornographic possibilities or practices.

Monogamy among men here typically is either a joke or a triumph of repression; their promiscuous intent and pulls, however quiet or well-behaved, remains very much alive, fed by mechanically wandering attention. Women at this stage are usually more inclined toward monogamy than men, mostly because it promises a certain security or semblance of solidity for them, although they know, in their heart of hearts, that they are chronically on the verge of being betrayed by their partners. Affairs occur frequently. There is deep confusion between romanticized lust and sexual love. Orgasm has excessive importance, to the point of turning everything that precedes it into foreplay.

Sex primarily serves egoity in me-centered relationships. Most couples here use sex as an escape or refuge from the rest of their life, assigning it to the labor of making them feel better or more secure. For many men here, marriage means, to whatever degree, a kind of entrapment, lightened by promiscuous fantasy and the promise of regular sex; and for more than a few women here, marriage is little more than legalized prostitution (trading sex for security, financial and otherwise). Power issues commonly find expression through sex at this stage; for men, egoic gratification is a typical payoff, and for women, better positional status and bargaining leverage.

Things are not much better in we-centered codependent couples. Sex is less risky (meaning that there are less affairs and less experimentation), but usually more boring, especially after a couple has been together for more than a few years. The lack of real challenge in the relationship, plus the suppression of emotional passion and intensity, simply makes for a flattened sexual life, no matter how many turn-on strategies are employed. Eroticism hasn't gone away, but has simply gone undercover.

There is more focus at this stage on using sex to stabilize the relationship; as such, sex is nicer, kinder, but usually not as juicy and exciting. There just isn't enough polarity between the partners to generate the intensity that is an essential ingredient of deep sex. The emphasis on not rocking the boat — the relation-ship — flattens arousal. Security is a priority, and sex has to fit into this. As in me-centered relationships, sex is kept separate from the rest of the relationship. Monogamy is more stable, but still lacks a solid foundation.

In we-centered coindependent couples, there's more passion, but without any increase in heart. The independence of each is paramount, and so sex has to serve this, providing pleasure, but nothing mind-blowing enough to blast through the partners' exaggerated attachment to their independence. Polarity at this stage is strong enough to keep sex alive, but not strong enough to really rock the couple. Sex is more out in the open than in we-centered codependent relationships, and is less impersonal and coarse than in me-centered couples, but still is chained to the obligation to make us feel better.

And being-centered relationships? Partners here approach sex already open, already at ease and happy, already fully connected to each other, so that sex is not expected to *produce* openness, happiness, or connection, but rather to simply be a mutually generated expression — and often also ecstatic intensification — of these.

Sex at this stage doesn't make love, but rather expresses, magnifies and celebrates love. The mix of raw openness, powerful polarity, deep friendship, unquestioned safety and commitment, unshakable love, and hyperbole-transcending connectedness generates a quality of sex far beyond what any sexual technology could produce. No pelvic or tantric headlocks here — just the wild, everfresh yes of love-ravished lust, as awake as it is passionate.

Chapter Twenty Seven

A FEW SUGGESTIONS FOR SEX IN INTIMATE RELATIONSHIP

1. Open Your Eyes

Be conscious before sex, during sex, and after sex. Open your eyes to whatever is going on during sex besides the erotic; don't pull away to thus see, but let your looking be as intimate as it is focused. Stay present, stay vital, and stay committed to being fully engaged with each other.

If you see or feel yourself and/or your partner getting mechanical, step in, interrupt, and redirect the energetic flow, making your connection with each other more important than any sexual payoff.

Have enough light in the room — a single candle may be enough — to be able to see each other's eyes. For at least some of the time, keep eye contact with each other, letting your gaze be open, relaxed, and present. Sometimes during orgasm, keep full eye-contact, allowing yourself total vulnerability and freedom of expression. At times when you gaze into each other's eyes, you will see only personality; other times, you will see far more; and sometimes you will see everything. Let it be.

When sex becomes an ecstatically intimate, wide-awake loving, we will find ourselves in a depth at once familiar and beyond all description, a depth inviting us to walk through it hand in hand, hearts as one, minds but pure space, our flesh but energy fluctuating between electrifyng joy and unshakable peace. Open eyes.

2. Stop Making Orgasm So Important

Orgasm tends to be as overrated as it is misunderstood.

First of all, orgasm is not necessarily equivalent to ecstasy. It is often not anything more than the pleasurable rupturing and dissolution of erotic buildup, having more to do with a craved maximizing of erotic sensation than with genuine sexual intimacy. When orgasm follows sex that was primarily engaged in for the purpose of making us feel better, then it is mostly just pleasurable release, however intense it might be.

Orgasm is ecstatic when sex is ecstatic, and sex is only ecstatic when we come to it *already* loose and happy, *already* open and unpressured, *already* unburdened by any craving to have something special occur. (By ecstasy, I mean an intensification and expansion of happiness, not situational happiness — or the kind of happiness that depends on something in particular occurring, like winning a load of money — but the happiness that is inherent to Being.)

We cannot stimulate ourselves into ecstasy, even through the most intensely arousing sexual rituals or practices. The very peak of sexual excitation positions us for the release for which we've been aching, the thrilling discharge of whatever tension that we may have sexually generated. Orgasm, the promised payoff, the eruption of the peak, the Big Moment, the little death, the all-too-brief break from mental chatter, the sleeping pill par excellence, and so on — but with whatever we might associate it, orgasm is not necessarily ecstasy. If what precedes orgasm is less than ecstatic, then orgasm is at best but a bolt or flood of intense pleasure, a few waves of delicious thrill, very soon to be but a cul-de-sac of quickly spent excitation.

Ecstasy is not addictive. Only when we have turned away from ecstasy do we get addictive, creating dependency-relationships with whatever promises to deliver to us some relatively convincing semblance of ecstasy. In the absence of ecstasy, eroticism holds immense appeal, with orgasm being its star attraction.

When sex is ecstatically loving, orgasm is not discontinuous with what precedes it, but rather is an explosively felt intensification of full-bodied mutual happiness, an overwhelmingly blissful explosion throughout our entire being, streaming, rushing, and expanding with delicious force and abandon as if from our very core, pouring and flooding up through our heart (sometimes even *beginning* there), both enveloping and expanding our body from the inside out, until we are but sentient energy in profoundly loving, indescribably intimate communion with our partner. Orgasm as such is inherently rejuvenating.

Typical orgasm, however, is very different. In men, it does not rejuvenate, but rather only drains (and here I'm talking about orgasm which includes ejaculation), regardless of its intensity. Orgasm for men is often no more than a discharge of excess or built-up energy, an emptying of tension, a pleasure-spasm soon followed by enervation and a dulling drowsiness. Orgasm cannot enliven us if love is not present, and nor can it fill the whole body if there is any holding back, physical or emotional or otherwise, anywhere in us. Even at the moment of ejaculation, many men (especially in me-centered and we-centered relationships) tend to control themselves, repressing their vulnerability, merely emptying themselves of their desire, no longer pumping any energy into a display of apparent intimacy. By not remaining heart-open and emotionally naked, they force the energy of orgasm to dissipate itself in their legs, pelvis, and head, thereby sedating their system.

Typical orgasm drains women in a different way. Its soporific or stress-discharging effect may still be present, but is usually not so strong or central as is an underlying dissatisfaction, a suddenly naked sense of emotional and perhaps also spiritual loneliness, which may lead to a longing for either more distraction (sexual and otherwise), or for some real intimacy. The pleasure and relief of orgasm may mask this, but usually not for long.

Don't try for bigger or better orgasms. Rather, do the necessary work to go into sex already loving, vital, and vulnerable. *Make connection with your partner priority*. Get naked and stay naked. Allow your sexual times with your partner to be not orgasm-aimed, but rather *orgasmic*, moment-to-moment sensually and sexually lovingly alive. Don't go for orgasms; let them come to you, and when they do, give yourself wholly over to them, even as you invite your partner into the heart of your joy.

3. Let the Whole Relationship Be Foreplay

In me-centered relationships, foreplay is a job, a preliminary, a warmup, a preparatory ritual, more often than not mechanical. In we-centered relationships, foreplay is still mostly a job, but is delivered with more care, being more of a mutually connected undertaking.

In being-centered relationships, by contrast, foreplay ceases to be a separate or preliminary practice. The whole relationship is foreplay. Each conversation, each touch, each greeting, each challenge, in some way keeps the juices flowing. There is no effort to be erotic, no turn-on strategies, no manipulation — but there *is* great passion, effortless and often instantaneous arousal, and a deep capacity for mutual ecstasy, unburdened by any pressure to get sexual.

The relationship during sex is the very same relationship outside of sex, lit by the same deep recognition of each other. Such profoundly loving recognition is the foundation for the deepest sex of all.

4. Be Emotionally Naked

Take off more than your clothes. Don't just settle for bare flesh meeting bare flesh. Get wet, and not just physically. The more open you and your partner are emotionally, the deeper and more life-giving the sex.

Be emotionally naked, and show it. Don't just say "I love you" dutifully or mechanically — say it (assuming that it is natural to say it at the time) from your core, sensing and expressing the essential significance of each word.

Get vulnerable and stay vulnerable. This is especially important for us men; if we do not allow ourselves to be vulnerable, then only part of us — mostly cranial and penile — will be participating. If we truly want depth, then we need to leave the shallow end of the pool, without necessarily knowing what we'll encounter as we venture forth.

Get your heart into being fully vulnerable; there is not a more powerful aphrodisiac than mutual full-blooded and totally unguarded love. When your heart is open and your belly is loose and your voice unrestricted, the energy that has built up in your genitals can flood upward through your belly into your heart, throat, skull, and beyond. The more emotionally open you are, the deeper your sexual experience will be.

Feeling and expressing an unqualified, emotionally naked yes! for your partner, along with a simultaneously arising gratitude and wild yet love-centered lust, enlivens the whole body and more, so that when sex gets going, its palette is our entire self.

5. Increase the Polarity

Assuming that there's already a deeply shared intimacy, the more male he is, the more female she will be, and vice versa. It is easy (and not uncommon!) to get more androgynous as we journey more fully into our spirituality; this may be fine when we're doing solitary practice or are in professional mode at work, but not so fine when it comes to our intimate relationship.

For men, it is crucial that they contact and fully embody their core adult masculinity, reclaiming their balls without losing touch with their heart, so that they are simultaneously capable of great erotic presence and equally great tenderness. As he becomes more fully present, more strongly anchored in love, integrity, and his essential masculinity, he becomes not only more trustworthy to his partner, but also more attractive, so that she can open more fully to him, with the result that their lovemaking becomes much, much more than just a mechanical ritual or exercise.

As women contact and embody their core adult femininity, bringing a deeply centered power to their heartfulness, they become more capable of opening fully; and at the same time, their inner radar will be so clear that any shift in their partner will be immediately obvious to them. If he, for example, loses some presence or gets a bit mechanical or goal-oriented during sex, she will call this to his attention without hesitation, giving him the gift of her fierce compassion, however gently she might deliver it.

There can be great polarity between immature lovers, but it is mostly just a polarity of *sensation*. Upping the stimulation can produce enough erotic tension to set off some powerful orgasms — but so what? A juicy fire — lots of heat, but usually not much light or genuine closeness. Intense sensation, however pleasurable, is not really all that satisfying, for it leaves out too much of us.

The polarity between being-centered partners can be mind-blowingly great, since it hypervividly highlights (and simultaneously celebrates) the differences between male and female in every dimension — which only increases the longing, the enormously rich longing, for the two to meet as deeply as they possibly can.

There's an indescribably sweet aching in this, for both lovers are keenly aware of how short their time is together, and the more intensely vivid the polarity between them, the more powerful and satisfying and illuminating their encounter.

6. Don't Separate Sex from the Rest of Your Relationship

What we do sexually may seem very different from what we do in the rest of our relationship, but it is in fact simply a reflection, however energetically magnified, of our overall relationship. What is not working in our relationship will show up in our sex life, no matter how much our sex life may seem to be a "solution" to or escape from the rest of our relationship. Once we stop trying to isolate our sexual relationship from the rest of our relationship — and deal skillfully with whatever's not working there — we become more conscious during sex, so that it becomes not only a time of deeply felt connection, erotic and otherwise, but also a time of discovering, uncovering, and recovering.

7. Connect Before, During, and After Sex

Instead of trying to find connection through sex with your partner, come to sex *already connected* — that is, already feeling intimate — with your partner. If you don't feel close to your partner, don't then go for sex, but rather mutually face and work through whatever's obstructing your closeness with each other.

If you start to lose connection during sex — as can happen when we slip into fantasy or try to make things go a certain way — interrupt whatever you're doing sexually, and let your partner know what is going on with you, and stay with it until you are both reconnected, even if this means not resuming your lovemaking. This is not about shaming or blaming, but about simply changing gears.

Staying connected after sex does not mean dutifully trying to be close, but rather making your connection with each other such a priority that you are held in the circle of each other's loving embrace, even when that circle expands infinitely.

Chapter Twenty Eight

THE WILD YES OF LOVE-RAVISHED LUST

Many men give love — or something *resembling* love — to get sex, and probably just as many women give sex to get love — or something *resembling* love. But in either case, sex is just doing time, having been sentenced to slave labor in the sweatshops of our neuroses.

When sex is employed as a means of distracting us from our suffering, sedating us and perhaps also providing us with a briefly convincing illusion of being truly connected, we are left out in the cold, no matter how heated our sex may be.

We may not want to see what we are *really* up to during sex, aside from pleasurably stimulating and consoling ourselves. We may not want to see the context within which we are operating before, during, and after sex. And we may not want to see that we don't want to seriously consider any of the above! However, if we pay conscious attention to ourselves and our partner in the midst of sexual engagement (beginning with the first signs of erotic interest and intensification) — which does *not* mean dissociating from our partner or from our own experience! — we have a chance to view not only the underpinnings of our suffering, but also our craving to escape from that suffering.

We will then literally catch ourselves in the act, realizing that what we tend to do sexually is often no more than an exaggeration of what we tend to do when we are not being sexual.

Sexual sanity and joy is not possible without a corresponding sanity and joy in the rest of our life.

There are many way of abusing our sexuality, not the least of which occurs when we try to spiritualize it, burdening it with metaphysical or tantric expectations, attempting to manipulate it into something "higher" or holier. But sex does not need to be the gateway to bliss or superconsciousness, but rather needs to be unchained from such "high" expectations (and their generally unacknowledged spiritual ambition), so that it can be naturally and spontaneously expressed, unpolluted by notions of "higher" or "lower."

Sex can be deeply, even profoundly, spiritual when we stop trying to engineer it into "higher" domains — all that's needed is deep mutual trust and passion, undressed love, full-blooded surrender, and no attachment to particular outcomes, as is epitomized by being-centered relationships.

The raw wonder and beauty in which we may then find ourselves immersed is not a familiar something, but an always-fresh arising and presence that cannot help but evoke in us a deep gratitude. We are then not knowers of the truly sacred, but rather lovers and intimates of it, pulsing together at an edge beyond which there is only Absolute Mystery. This asks for partners for whom sex is deeply intimate merging, devotional lust, sacred bodyplay, ecstasy in the flesh, lit through and through with awakened love and ease.

Sex is neither salvation nor consolation. Do not encumber it with hope. Do not become insensitive to its seasons, its tides, its silences, its molten mystery and edgeless invitation.

And do not cheapen it with unnecessary stimulation-strategies — if we need to fantasize (or immerse our attention in titillating inner theater) in order to have "good" sex, then we are not displaying interest in sexual intimacy and depth, but rather only in mind-games whose primary purpose is to maximize not only pleasurable sensation, but also distraction from the more unpleasant aspects of what we may be feeling with our partner.

If sexual passion does not simply arise out of mutual love and connection, then why force it, why induce it, why fantasize or rub ourselves into it, why put our sexuality in a pelvic — or spiritual — headlock?

The point is not to "make" love, but rather *to make room for love*, letting such openness be the ground, the anchor, the unfabricated basis, the animating center of whatever we do.

Here, sex does not promise joy, but instead *begins* with joy, with love, with uncensored intimacy, with deep trust and faith in the unfathomable openness of the Real.

Here, sex is wild yet profoundly connected love, love in the ecstatically intimate raw, love both nakedly primal and exquisitely tender, effortlessly transparent to Being and simultaneously rooted in uncaged passion, blazing through both the personal and the transpersonal, no longer burdened by any expectation that it make us feel better or more secure or whole.

In the womanly wilds of you
I lose face without losing touch
Coming alive in the depths of so much
These sky-ribbed waves of ecstasy
Upon which we ride so fluid and free
Are the waves of which we're made
Every last one divinely okayed

Both together and alone
We reach beyond the known
Until there is but endless light
Clearer than the clearest insight
Twin flames effortlessly awake
Shining through every heartbreak

This, this is love's doing
The love here before the beginning
The love that expands without thinning
Only this love can bend the light
Only this love can hold all the history
Only this love can hold every view
Only this love can shape the light
Shapes like you and me
Transparencies unveiled
Divinely detailed

V. Bringing It All Together

Chapter Twenty Nine

COMMITMENT

Women want it; men don't.

Women use their wiles to get it; men use theirs to avoid it. For women, it spells security; for men, the loss of freedom.

At least this is how it usually is looked upon culturally, whether in midday kitchen chats, bars, or the routines of stand-up comedians. And just what is this it?

Commitment.

In its early stages, relational commitment is just a weightier version of a New Year's Resolution — a promise or deal that's frequently made under questionable conditions (inner, outer, or both), conditions rooted, however indirectly, in some kind of coercion or pressure overlaid with an appeal to what is supposedly higher or more mature in us.

Of course, commitment of this sort usually fails, for the same reasons that most New Year's Resolutions don't make it past the end of January: Our heart is not really in it, and there are opposing forces in us that were not sufficiently taken into account when we made, or forced ourselves to make, our "commitment."

Mature commitment, however, is a *very* different thing, rooted not in the enthusiasm of ill-considered shoulds or similar hype, but in an integral, well-seasoned knowingness.

In immature relationships, commitment usually signals a gain for the woman, and a loss for the man. She weaves her web; he gets sucked into it. She casts her line; he gets hooked. And so on. This way of thinking runs deep in our culture, framing women as having power over men; to take but one example, men all too often automatically blame women for whatever erotic interest arises in them toward women, as so succinctly illustrated by she-as-agent declarations like: "She put a spell on me" or "She makes me hard" or "She gets me all hot."

(The largely unquestioned helplessness of men — whether drooling, suave, or just plain geeky — in the presence of feminine allure has potentially dangerous implications, especially when it contrasts with a man's investment in maintaining a self-image that's free of helplessness or powerlessness. In short, if she "brings out the beast in me," I may then feel justified, however slightly, in "preying upon" or "pouncing upon" her. After all, was it not *she* who got that "animality" in me all stirred up in the first place?)

The fact that being committed has more than one meaning is especially relevant here. In some cases, "being committed" means being taken, often *against our will*, to a psychiatric institution, presumably because of our psychoemotional instability, delusional leanings, and so on. And do not most immature men apply much the same take — that "being committed" means we're being taken in, or are even "crazy" — to being committed to an intimate relationship?

At the me-centered stage of relationship, commitment is seen only for what it can do for us. It fits our conditioning. We may think that we are committing to another, but in fact our apparent commitment to that other is permitted only because it gives us something that we crave, like a sense of security or belonging or alignment with familial/cultural expectations. So we come first, with our relationship existing mostly only to feed and support us. However selfless or self-sacrificing commitment may seem to be here, it remains at essence a selfish undertaking, an ego-governed contract or deal.

What's primarily running the relationship at this stage is the *conditioning* of both partners, the mutual enmeshing of which might initially feel satisfying — in that "we" seem to fit with each other — but sooner or later, as the darker or more obviously neurotic elements of both partners' conditioning emerge more fully, the relationship gets stuck, survival strategies take the field, and things generally degenerate.

For example, the pleasing behavior Ann developed as a child in order to survive her brutal father was initally a huge plus for her partner, John, (who was neglected as a child and grew up craving being taken care of), but later, as the underlying dissociative behavior Ann used as a child (to remove herself from the violence she endured from her father) more and more clearly surfaces, John finds less comfort in her pleasing behavior, and pushes for more connection, not seeing that his doing so only drives Ann deeper into her dissociative tendencies. And on it goes.

As high as the divorce rate is, it would probably be even higher if all those who are committed to putting up with deadened, erosive, or abusive relationships were to step forward and honor their deeper needs.

At the we-centered codependent stage of relationship, commitment is viewed not only for what it can do for us, but also — and often more importantly — for what it can do for our relationship. Each of us remains important, but the overlap between us, the intersubjective space that we cocreate and co-occupy, is given central importance.

That space, that arena of connectedness, is still largely made up of our shared conditioning, but our commitment to keeping our relationship together is much stronger. We have moved from being two cults of one enmeshed with each other to more or less a cult of two (and here, I don't mean "cult" in the automatically pejorative, sensationalistic manner of the mainstream media — which are themselves often quite cultic in their exclusion of anything that *seriously* challenges them — but rather only a self-enclosed entity all but impermeable to outside feedback and inside dissension).

In we-centered coindependent relationships, commitment tends to be less cultically structured. The we-space is still very important, but can be, for the first time, stood apart from to a sufficient degree to be actually seen. Both partners are committed not only to taking care of their relationship, but also of themselves.

A true interdependence has not yet fully emerged, being overwhelmed by the couple's exaggerated focus on maintaining their independence within the relationship, but it has begun to arise. Commitment is now more than a should, but still less than a natural foundational support for the relationship.

At the being-centered relational stage, commitment to the relationship both deepens the relationship and energetically expands it beyond the partners, emanating out to touch many, and not necessarily deliberately. Such relationship feels good to be around. The couple at this stage may not be working in fields that brings them into contact with many others, nor have a particularly active social life, but the very presence and quality of their bond nevertheless radiates out, benefitting those who are within its range.

The me-centered relationship does not serve others to any significant degree; the we-centered codependent can under very limited conditions, and the we-centered coindependent under less limited conditions; and the being-centered cannot help but serve others — it's an utterly natural byproduct of their intimacy. Theirs is the freedom of having no choice in this. They're not *trying* to serve others, but simply cannot do otherwise.

Real commitment in a relationship cannot be forced.

If it is, it is not commitment, but just *submission*. Real commitment is an organic process, unfolding and ripening as we get closer and closer to our beloved other — and to our own core of being. Our moment-to-moment encounters and exchanges ready the soil; the seeds of commitment are already there, needing only suitable ground, care, and timing. There is no point in planting seeds in frozen or unprepared ground, as those in more immature stages of relatedness are prone to doing, in their enthused blending with another.

When we mature, we both take our time and do not waste any time, making haste slowly. We may experience an enormous amount in a short time of being together, but we ensure that we allow proper digestion and assimilation of what we have experienced together.

No matter how close we feel to the other in the early stages of meeting, we don't get lost in futurizing (as epitomized by premature planning), finding all that we need in being deeply and consistently *present* with the other. Simply being with the other like this allows a *natural* commitment to emerge, a commitment that fits us *as we are*, rather than fitting us to what we could or might hope to be.

Don't rush commitment, and don't put it off. Ask yourself how ready you *truly* are for it, and to what degree, if any, your wanting it is based on your conditioning (both familial and cultural).

Don't make a goal out of commitment, remembering that we're always already committed to something, including our avoidance of commitment.

To commit is to take, and keep taking, a stand that needs to be taken, while not submitting to ersatz integrity (that is, staying with a stand when circumstances make it clear that something else is called for, such as when our partner remains consistently abusive toward us and we stay because of our original commitment to stay).

Integrity and commitment are closely linked. Without integrity, there is no real commitment, but only promises and reassurances. Without integrity, our word means little, and if what we say cannot be consistently trusted, how can there be any depth of intimacy?

The fact that a commitment can be broken or replaced by a more central commitment (e.g., our commitment not to steal may be overridden by our commitment to feed our children) does not mean that commitment ought to be taken lightly! If we are not ready to take a stand, we would do best to wait until we *are* ready, so that our stand is stably grounded and established in us.

Commitment is an open-eyed, ongoing, and resolutely empowered yes to a well-considered choice. It is more than a promise, unpolluted by maybe's and loopholes. When we are truly committed to another, we can be counted upon to keep our word: We do what we say we're going to do, and when we cannot, we clearly and openly and without delay communicate *that*, without in any way dishonoring our bond with our partner. Commitment to another includes many other commitments, such as being present no matter what's happening.

Real commitment is much more than just meeting another halfway. There's a Zeno paradox about crossing a room by going half the distance, and then half that distance, ad infinitum — which means we never completely cross the room. Going more than halfway cuts through this; if we and our intimate other are both doing this, we not only engage in more and more overlap — deepening our intersubjectivity — but *do* get to the other side, so that we can include and benefit from the entire space between us.

In any commitment, we are making a choice not to make a bunch of *other* choices. That is, we are embracing a particular set of limitations. This will seem entrapping to the immature, but not to the mature.

For example, being confined to one woman may appear very narrowing to an immature man, once his honeymoon with her is over; with little novelty left (other than that rubbed into being through pornographic proclivity), and with little capacity to take the relationship deeper, he almost inevitably loses interest in her (although, ironically, he was never really that interested in *her*).

By contrast, being confined to one partner is far from narrowing to a mature man. He finds, and keeps finding, his partner remarkably interesting; his familiarity with her only affirms and deepens the mystery of her for him.

His being limited to her is his freedom, for through his ever-deepening intimacy with her, he touches far more than just another human being. Some might say that he has sacrificed breadth for depth, and they are right, but only *partially* right.

Initially, there's little breadth but considerable depth; later on, as more depth is accessed, and he starts to experience archetypal dimensions of the feminine through his partner, there is more breadth, and therefore a wider embrace of the feminine; and still later on, as a dimensionless depth of being is accessed, there's much more breadth, much more of an encompassing sense of her, until she is, however fleetingly or subtly, experienced as none other than him, at which point relationship is but sacred communion.

Commitment makes relational intimacy possible, and relational intimacy deepens commitment, until there is no difference between commitment to our own healing and awakening, and commitment to our intimate relationship.

Immature commitment contracts and entraps us; mature commitment expands and liberates us.

Freedom through limitation.

Chapter Thirty

THE NEED FOR SAFETY IN INTIMATE RELATIONSHIP

To go truly deep in an intimate relationship, we need to feel safe with our partner. We need to know — and know with our whole being — that we can *trust* them, and not just when we are with them.

This is a trust based not on thinking that we should trust them, but rather on feeling right to our core their *trustworthiness* — their integrity, their reliability, their commitment to remaining present under all conditions, their passion for accessing love, depth, and freedom with and through us. (See the following chapter for more on trust.)

If we cannot count on our partner to consistently take good care of the container of our relationship — as when energy is leaked through cracks created by erotically wandering attention — then we will find there is only so deep we can go with them.

If one partner is chronically calling the whole relationship into question every time there's a fight or conflict, then the other is probably going to become wary of opening fully.

Less safety means more shallows.

Making the ground of our relationship unnecessarily unstable — as when certain boundaries are overridden or trivialized in the name of "freedom" — keeps our relationship from being as deep and fulfilling as it could be. The point isn't to create a fortress of security, but to literally be a safe place for our partner to let go of playing it safe. Feeling safe is much more than just feeling secure!

Real safety creates an atmosphere in which we can give our all without giving ourselves away.

Real safety makes room for a radically deep sharing of all that we are. Without it, we may seem to be free to go where we could not otherwise go, but such freedom — in its relative superficiality — is actually far more limiting than is the freedom that arises in the presence of genuine safety between intimates.

The safer I feel with you, the deeper I can go with you. The safer I feel with you, the deeper the *risks* I can take with you. The safer I feel with you, the deeper and more fulfilling the passions are between us; anger becomes a guardian of intimacy, lust a magnifier of intimacy, and ecstasy a celebration of intimacy.

Real safety gives us room to show up in all our colors.

Such safety gives us permission to be in as much pain as we actually are, thereby making possible the healing we need in order to come fully alive, the healing through which we are awakened by all things. What joy, what benediction, what grace, to share this in the dynamic safety possible in an intimate relationship!

Chapter Thirty One

DEEPENING TRUST

For me to trust you means that I — having consistently witnessed your integrity and reliability — have an abiding confidence that you will continue to manifest such qualities. Trust as such is not an a priori stance, but a *result.*

The deeper our mutual trust, the deeper our relationship can go, so long as that trust is rooted not in naiveté — naive or blind trust is not really trust, but rather just a cocktail of foolhardiness and hope — but in a mutuality that's anchored in transparency, integrity, and love. Trust should not be automatically given; it must be earned.

In the beginning, we may be enamored by another's better qualities, and want to give that one our trust — especially if there's a romantic infusion of hope and lust — but we'd do best to withhold giving our *full* trust until enough time has passed to see the other in action in a variety of circumstances.

If our bullshit detector is turned down to too low a volume — perhaps because we don't want our romantic trance to be interrupted — we will probably get sloppy in giving our trust, selling it for a few baubles of feel-good attention.

Seeing how our partner operates when things get rough provides a clear indicator of their trustworthiness. Are they worthy of our trust? We need to find this out, rather than just believing it from the start, out of some naive or romantic notion that we should thus believe.

Without a strongly anchored mutual trust, intimate relationship mostly remains stranded in the shallows, regardless of its excursions to deeper territory. When I ask most couples if they trust each other, there is often some hesitation before they say yes — that is, if they even say yes. A hesitant yes is not a full yes; we may be saying yes because we want to trust our partner, or think that we should. But a yes that is animated or bullied into being by any form of "should" is not a full yes.

Part of building trust is an honest, in-depth sharing of how we have been less than trustworthy in our past. This is not about re-shaming ourselves for old transgressions and stupidities, but rather about sharing what has happened openly, vulnerably, and in the spirit of establishing a healthy foundation with our partner. No secrets. This can be a painful process, but it is necessary. Not every detail is needed, but enough need to be provided so as to provide a sufficiently clear picture and sense of what happened.

As we do this, it is crucial that we uncover — perhaps with our partner's assistance — the prevailing patterns underlying our past behavior. Some of these patterns may truly be things of the past, but others may still be very much present, however much they may be under wraps. These must be revealed so that they can be worked with; this is not about shaming each other, but rather is about not keeping anything from each other. Doing so is an act of deep trust.

Another part of building trust is to openly share our *mistrust*. We might be tempted to act as if we trust our partner with something or someone, but if we don't, to whatever degree, we need to share *that*. To thus share our mistrust is actually an act of trust. If we are on the receiving end of this, we need to remain as open as possible; if we belittle or otherwise shame our partner for daring to mistrust us, they will be less likely to want to share their mistrust with us in the future.

Without mutual trust, there will not be enough safety in the relationship to go truly deep. For example, a couple may, regardless of their love for each other, get sloppy when anger arises — becoming hostile, sarcastic, passive aggressive, blaming, and so on — thereby becoming less than a safe space for each other; they may still open to each other, but it will only go so far, simply because there's not enough safety, or well-rooted trust, to go further.

We don't want to be at a relational edge and not know if our partner can be trusted to hold the line secure. This is why it is so crucial to identify any cracks in the container of the relationship. Even occasional sarcasm can generate such cracks, however thin or slight they may be. Aggression cracks the container, as does contempt and a lack of integrity. Infidelity all but destroys the container, as does violence.

Mature couples are deeply and consistently committed to keeping their relational container free from cracks. The container can be transparent, permeable, even immeasurably expansive, but it is nonetheless still a container, a protected space wherein freedom is found not through escaping the container, but rather through viewing and treating it as a sanctuary of love, awakening, and transformation.

If I am untrustworthy in certain areas, do not override your concerns just because I am so wonderful in other ways; that is, do not let my good points obscure or marginalize my not-so-good points. Relate to me as I am, rather than having a relationship with — or being seduced by — my trustworthiness potential.

The better the relationship, the deeper the trust, and vice versa. When I trust you fully, I can open with you until I am but openness, sentient openness. When I trust you fully, then our relationship becomes a dynamic crucible for healing, awakening, and relational deepening, so that no matter what arises, it is workable. When I trust you fully, I become more alive, more fleshed-out, more conscious, more brave, more curious and caring, letting our relationship carry me beyond what I have taken myself to be.

When we are truly connected, even the arising of disconnection is okay. In fact, trusting each other with our disconnectedness only deepens our mutual trust. The deepest trust of all is but lucid opening to reality in the raw, at once rooted in and generating a sublimely solid faith, a faith that holds steady in even the stormiest relational times.

When it is clearly time to trust — as when our partner has consistently demonstrated his or her trustworthiness — do so even if you are afraid to do so. Better at such times to have trusted and gotten hurt, than not to have trusted.

Chapter Thirty Two

GETTING HONEST ABOUT HONESTY

Honesty is generally taken to be an unquestioned good in intimate relationships. However, before we attach to the practice of honesty the status of a rock-solid or not-to-be-questioned virtue, let us ask: Honest about what?

If we, for example, are being honest about what we want — upfront, clear, straightforward — are we *also* being honest about what's driving such want, or about what we're hoping that our honesty will bring us, or about what we are, for strategic or less than noble reasons, *not* being upfront, clear, and straightforward?

So let us be honest about honesty: There is more to it than meets the eye and ear. I may tell you that I want you to be honest with me no matter what you are feeling, giving you appreciation when you let me know, for example, that you are angry at me — and I may assume that I'm doing a good thing here, in encouraging you to be more outfront, more emotionally transparent and expressive.

At the same time, however, I might be doing this in part because it allows me to stay in control; however benignly or subtly I am overseeing your state, I am nevertheless still *overseeing* it, making sure that the primary focus on what is not working so well in our relationship is on *you*, and remains on you.

Now let's take this a bit further, reversing the roles: You may say, in apparent honesty, that you want me to be honest with you, even if I think that doing so will upset you, but you are not actually being all that honest, if only because you are not openly and clearly sharing — and therefore not being honest about — your underlying motivation for wanting me not to hold back from you. It's not that you *really* want me not to thus hold back, but rather that you want to be in a position where *you* are calling the shots, however obliquely.

And there's more: Even if you were actually honest about your wanting to be in control, you would need to make sure that your delivery of this was not being fueled by the desire to garner some strokes — or some kind of advantage — for your "humble" confession. That is, you would need to make sure that you were not, through such self-disclosure, still trying to be in control, if only through steering my response in a direction you approve of or desire.

To truly expose your wanting to be in control — which would be an act of radical honesty — you would have to let go of your attachment to any expected outcome, which would, of course, leave you vulnerable and, yes, potentially *out-of-control.*

How honest can we be if we are operating from our conditioning, and don't recognize that we are doing so?

There are levels of honesty. We cannot be significantly honest at a level with which we do not have any intimacy. Unfortunately, we may nonetheless still act as if we are indeed being honest at that level, when in fact we are not capable of doing so. This means, among other things, that we need to recognize where we are standing, and have the humility to admit where we cannot yet stand (such admission being a capacity that does not begin until we're at least at a we-centered stage of relationship). No shame in this — just genuinely self-revealing honesty, the honesty to openly admit our inability to maintain honesty at certain levels (and perhaps also under certain conditions).

An example: We have the habit of snapping at our partner over trivial matters, while reassuring her after each snapping episode that we'll not do it again. If we were being honest, we'd say that we know we'll very likely do it again, and that we also know that we may once again claim that we'll not do it again. This is not about cutting ourselves excess slack, but about being honest (including about our dishonesty regarding our claim of not snapping anymore). There is no reason why we can't also work out with our partner a practice which we can do (and that she can remind us to do) when we're entering snapping territory. Honoring where we are means, among other things, being straight about it, including our less-than-honorable tendencies.

Honesty and honor not only share the same linguistic ancestry, but are also deeply intertwined. Can we have honor without honesty? I don't think so. To be truly honest with others is to honor them, to not in any way abuse the sanctity of their being; although we may not say *everything* to them, what we do say is truthful, and what we don't say in all likelihood does not really *need* to be said (at least at that time). This is the essence of real honesty, infused with self-illuminating discernment and genuine care for the other.

Someone once said that an honest politician is one who, when bought, stays bought. Let's do whatever we can to raise our capacity for honesty to a higher level, beginning with being honest about our dishonesty as best we can. In all honesty, there probably is not a much better place to begin.

In me-centered relationships, honesty is very -easily corrupted and is self-serving; in we-centered codependent relationships, honesty is not so easily corrupted and is narrowly we-serving; in we-centered coindependent relationships, honesty is only mildly corruptible, and is both self-serving and we-serving; and in being-centered relationship, honesty is not corruptible, and serves the highest good of all, arising from a dynamically awakened moral core.

Chapter Thirty Three

PSYCHOTHERAPY AND PRACTICES FOR COUPLES

We do not reach mature monogamy without working for it, and an essential part of such work is psychotherapy — whether done on an individual basis, or as a couple, or both — as well as practices that address and help us to make good use of various elements in our relationship.

Before proceeding further, I need to say that I consider psychotherapy (at best, a *more-than-just-intellectual integral psychotherapy*, working in depth and fitting detail with mind, body, emotions, spirituality, and relevant cultural factors) as essential at some point for *everyone.*

Yes, there are other avenues of self-exploration and personal growth besides psychotherapy, but some quality time spent with a suitably skilled professional examining and directly working with your conditioning, reactivity, and psychoemotional logjams is invaluable, if only because doing so can both illuminate and deeply address tendencies — *and* also the roots of such tendencies — that other modes of self-exploration (such as lifestyle coaching, personal growth seminars, and mindfulness training) tend to bypass or only superficially address.

Unfortunately, there still remains in our culture a shaming that often accompanies one's going to psychotherapy, especially for men. I often say to men who are beginning some psychotherapy that it takes balls to do so; later, we will sometimes talk about how the percentage of men doing psychotherapy tends to decrease as corporate and political status increases, so that those who are "at the top" are usually those who have done the least in-depth work on themselves. After all, how many sitting or would-be Presidents would admit to having done psychotherapy? Probably none (Bill Clinton's belated "pastoral counseling" being an anticlimactic exception, following his public shaming), as doing so would very likely seriously damage their credibility in the eyes of many.

I recall working with some top-level corporate men, and having them refer to me — as they apparently "had to" among their colleagues — as their "executive coach," rather than as their psychotherapist or even counselor, as if admitting to doing some psychotherapy was nothing more than a sign of having failed. Whatever their status or power, they were in shame's chains.

Having done some individual psychotherapy before our relationship began may be sufficient, or we may need some more as our relationship progresses. If we have each done enough prior to our relationship — and the measure of this is both in the depth of our self-knowledge and in our capacity to behave sanely in the midst of difficulties — we may not need any couples' counseling. At the same time, though, if difficulties arise in our relationship that we are not satisfactorily resolving, then we would be wise to do some couples' counseling as soon as possible. Be fussy in picking a psychotherapist who works with couples, but not so fussy that you talk yourselves out of doing any couples' counseling!

It can also be useful to do not just individual and couples psychotherapy, but also, if at all possible, some psychotherapy-including groupwork, both with and without our partner. Groupwork, at its most beneficial, includes not only the best of individual session work, but also abundant opportunities for the kind of healing and breakthrough (involving not just our present, but also our past) made possible in the dynamics of a safe-to-go-really-deep *interactive* environment. And what might these opportunities be? Consider the following description of a "typical" morning of groupwork...

After a greeting and brief introduction from me, the ten participants (sitting in a circle) take turns introducing themselves, saying, among other things, a bit about what they are having trouble dealing with and what they are hoping to get from being in the group. Inevitably, several get quite stirred up doing so. When everyone has had their turn, I begin working with one person (who usually steps forward with little or no invitation from me).

For a few minutes, I gather relevant information from that person, zeroing in on what is troubling or challenging them, and then begin deepening the work, through whatever intuitively fits at the moment, be it emotional deepening, psychodrama, conscious movement, guided meditation, or bodywork combined with psychotherapeutic direction. This usually brings about considerable energetic and emotional opening and expression, along with fitting insights.

The work may finish with that person, now considerably more open, returning to their place in the circle, or perhaps facing the group and deepening their contact with everyone, while mining their work for further insights into their life. I may then discuss what's just happened, emphasizing that each person's work is, in a very real sense, everyone's work, and encouraging everyone to let themselves, as much as possible, fully feel each person's work, and not to suppress what they're feeling while another is working.

Often the next person who comes forward to work has been deeply stirred by the first person's work and opening. By the time I've worked with the second participant, the whole group has come together, providing an ever-deepening environment for healing and awakening. When a piece of work is particularly moving, obviously affecting most in the group, I'll sometimes have them gather around the person who has just worked (and who may be sitting in the middle of the room or lying down on a mat), close their eyes, and stay there for a while, during which time I may play some fitting music, or Diane (my wife and assistant in the group) may sing.

After that's done, I may work with a third participant, or maybe with two participants (perhaps a couple, or perhaps two others who share a similar issue), or have some group discussion. Things are wide open now. The group has become a sanctuary for very deep work, without trying to be so. There's plenty of anger, tears, passion, and laughter. There's an unspoken but clear permission for everyone to be in as much pain as they actually are. I'm often amazed at this point to look at the clock and see that only an hour or so has gone by.

More work follows: Someone exposes and works with a difficult relationship they've had or are in, and as they do so, others who have been in or are in a similar bind gain insight and inspiration for dealing with that bind; someone else works with a feeling of isolation they keep having, exploring its roots and cutting through their isolation, and as they do so, everyone else feels more connected; someone else who feels powerless does deep work regarding this, eventually contacting a place of such power in themselves that everyone cannot help but celebrate with them; and so on.

In this kind of groupwork, one participant's work can catalyze others' work to a depth very difficult to otherwise access. The sharing of such work, level upon level, in an environment of intimate safety and trust is as liberating as it is practical, as heart-opening as it is empowering, as integration-promoting as it is clarifying.

Initially, the opportunity to self-disclose is often shyly or reluctantly approached, but after a short while, opening thus becomes not a burden, but a natural ease, a liberating exposure. Such a revealing of self does not necessarily mean having no boundaries, but in fact often is about opening to and clarifying the need for clearer, stronger boundaries.

When we can be open about being closed, compassionately present with our resistance to doing our work, we are not so far from being what we are seeking. When one person in a group does this, all usually feel a deepening inner permission to do the same, shedding "shoulds" and tuning in to what really matters. This is not to uncritically praise groupwork (for it has its own pathological possibilities, such as the overriding of individual needs by group needs), but to highlight the very real benefits that it can so abundantly supply.

I encourage everyone to share their intuitions and feelings after (and occasionally during) a participant's work. Toward the end of the morning session, I usually have participants sit in pairs, and lead them through improvised dyadic exercises (like spontaneously completing incomplete sentences while maintaining eye contact with each other). We almost always finish with a group circle, during which I'll teach a little meditation, and then have everyone let their voices flow out as I put something suitable on the stereo. Ten or so minutes later, and the morning session is over...

(Diane and I especially enjoy the couples groups we offer [usually 3-day groups for 5 couples only], which feature not only the kind of work described above [for each member of the couple], but also face-to-face work for each couple, work which is highly beneficial not only for the couple doing the work, but also for the other couples observing. As each couple exposes and works with their relational challenges, the other couples find an increasing capacity to do the same.)

Now, what about relationship-enhancing practices? If we're doing these (as perhaps garnered from self-help books or seminars) without having done any psychotherapy, then whatever good we are getting from doing them is likely going to be strongly limited by the lack of in-depth exploration and conditioning-exposure that is provided by skilled psychotherapy.

For example, we may be doing a practice that is supposed to increase our male-female polarity (that is, generate more charge, sexual and otherwise, between us and our partner), but might through such a practice only unwittingly reinforce our aggression (usually in the man) or passivity/seductiveness (usually in the woman), while thinking that we are somehow enhancing our masculinity or femininity. If we had, however, done some quality psychotherapy prior to this, we would be far less likely to let this practice reinforce our neuroses (and might then not even need to do such a practice).

Competent psychotherapy provides fitting practices — tailored both for individual and couples work — that *directly* stem from the deep work done in sessions. As couples engage in a particular practice (such as mindfully and firmly interrupting their own and each other's reactive tendencies), their psychotherapist can, after seeing how they are doing with their practice, modify and fine-tune it, or perhaps come up with a better one for them.

If both partners have done enough psychotherapy — as perhaps best demonstrated by their consistently mature approach to each other and to their own conditioning — they will benefit even more from doing various couples practices, so long as they do not engage in them mechanically. For example, if they have some difficulty expressing anger to each other, they can do practices that address this (such as getting passionate in expressing their anger while remaining responsible and compassionately attuned to the other while doing so), knowing that there is sufficient safety in the relationship to handle — and benefit from — such intensity.

And what about practices that do not come from psychotherapy? If we have done some psychotherapy, it's fine to experiment with these, whether they originate in self-help seminars or psychology books or spiritual undertakings. (And even if we haven't done any psychotherapy, such practices may get us going in that direction, by bringing to our attention some of our less-flattering qualities or by catalyzing unexpected openings in us.) Going for long walks together; intentionally giving what we want to receive; meditating while facing each other; not permitting sexual mechanicalness — these and other practices can be immensely helpful in deepening and strengthening our relationship. What matters is that we do them *fully*. If they don't work, or don't work all that well, and we've stayed with them for a while, then it's fine to drop them. Staying too long with a practice is as just as much of a mistake as leaving a practice too soon.

As a couple matures, the need to do couple-oriented practices diminishes, until there are no such practices that *need* to be done, simply because what needs to be done gets done without any reliance on them. But beware of trying to reach this point too quickly! The goal is *not* to not need to do any couple practices, but to do whatever work is necessary to reach such a point.

And such work necessarily includes a deep dip into psychotherapy and couple practices, along with employing the only real shortcut in healing work: realizing that there are no shortcuts. Most of us would love to have the benefits of a profound transformation of being without having to do the required work — such a fastfood mentality regarding work on ourselves needs to be supplanted by a healthier outlook, one that allows for proper digestion and integration.

I could list a number of highly effective practices, but these already have been described in earlier chapters, embedded in relevant detail and fitting context, so I will only recommend one practice here: Read each chapter of this book outloud with your partner, then discuss it thoroughly, and take on for an agreed-upon period its practices or, if no practices are suggested, cocreate some of your own based upon your mutual reading and discussion, and stick with them for an agreed-upon period. And only take on practices that are clearly doable!

After the psychotherapy and after the formal practices, you will come to realize that your *entire* relationship is a practice in the most sacred sense: Together you are creating a sanctuary for a kind of intimacy that has perhaps never been so needed, an intimacy in which "I"-centered reality and it's "us versus them" mentality is held in non-injurious perspective by a we-centered reality that eventually goes far beyond a "we" of just two, leaving us in the being-centered reality of mature monogamy.

Mature monogamy is not itself a practice, but what prepares the way for it requires commitment to various practices, especially those that arise from the kind of opening and insight possible through a truly integral psychotherapy.

Chapter Thirty Four

LOVE, AND A DEEPER LOVE

Love is not enough to make an intimate relationship work, but without love, there is no possibility of intimate relationship.

Only love can hold it all; only love has room for it all; only love is vast enough to include it all. Everything covered in this book can be held in love's presence — hence this chapter, inviting you to make even more room for what you have already read and taken in, so that it might more fully ripen in you.

Love is a great wonder and mystery to which we are inexorably drawn; we may have our heads aimed down toward troughs — whether material, psychological, or spiritual — of promised satisfaction, and there we may feed and make do for a while, but sooner or later we look up, with dissatisfaction running down our chin and disappointment wringing out our spine, and once again reach out for love, gradually eliminating greed and desperation from our reach, reaching with less and less hesitation, slowly but surely becoming pure reaching, finally *being* that for which we are reaching. Love — initially the goal, but eventually the foundation.

Love calls us, at first by our given name, then by our true name, and finally through all that is. It is an invitation that will not disappear. Love calls us home, not caring how long we have wandered, nor how long we have forgotten, nor how long our list of flaws may be. Nothing satisfies like love. As it *truly* is, it has no end, no bounds; it is without limitation. And, miracle of miracles, love is also right here, less than a breath away, ever awaiting our undressed attention, inviting us to embody and live and *be* it through everything — *everything* — that we do.

Although love may include attraction, it is more than attraction; love may include appetite, but is more than appetite; love may include kindness, but is more than kindness; love may include surrender, but is more than surrender; and so on. *Eros, philos, agapé*; love of food, love of sports, love of ideas, love of erotic play, love of God, love beyond love; puppy-dog love, fanatic love, unrequited love, ecstatic love, sacrificial love, down-in-the-dirt love and love sublime — so many facets and faces of love, so many forms and ways of loving, experientially so palpably obvious and definitionally so hard to corral, let alone pin down.

The state and practice of expansively felt, openly caring communion, whether with one or many or all that is — this is love.

Love is self-illuminating, life-affirming, supremely healing embrace, the heartbeat of real intimacy, the gratitude-suffused intuition and honoring of everywhere-present sacredness. I cannot say enough about love, but I will, of course, try.

Love simultaneously binds and liberates. It is, whatever its chains, the deepest freedom. It is both our birthright and deepest challenge.

Let's briefly jump to the Big Picture: Love is fundamentally just Absolute Mystery (and to name it thus does not mean that I *know* what it is!) openly and knowingly embracing itself through every possible manifestation of itself on every possible scale.

The *personalizing* of this is the essence of intimate relationship — we know ourselves through the other, ultimately recognizing right to our marrow that what's looking through our eyes at our partner is none other than what's looking through our partner's eyes at us. Prior to this, there are plenty of layers to see, feel, and permit an ever-deepening transparency.

Through love we eventually wake up, but it is a necessarily challenging journey, asking that we face, deal with, and move through *everything* within us that is in the way of love.

Relationships easily get stuck and lost in the melodramatics of intimate entanglement, but it is nonetheless possible for a relationship to reach sufficient transparency and openness so as to be able connect with what is beyond it, through full-blooded, deeply committed participation in that very relationship.

And how? By allowing ourselves to get so close that we cannot help but get *deeply* attached, and also (and just as importantly!) by simultaneously loving so strongly, so intensely, so fully — *especially* when things are really difficult — that we cease turning away from that in us (and others) which we ordinarily would have shunned, ostracized, or disowned.

However fierce love might have to be to deal with certain situations, it does *not* exclude.

When our heart breaks and we do not go to pieces, nor get bitter and twisted, we are in love's neighborhood. When we give what we most want to be given, we are on love's doorstep. When we truly realize that what we do to another we do to ourselves, we are in love's living room. When we include in the circle of our reach all that we are, we are in love's crucible. When we are in love's fire, and surrender to it without shrinking ourselves, making good use of both its heat and its light, we deepen our capacity to literally *be* love. Home is where the heart forever is.

At a personal level, love is basically the state of openly embracing and compassionately resonating with another's being. When this is attempted through the abandoning of personal boundaries, however, love is all but gone, obscured by the resulting fusion (soon to be *con*fusion) that commonly characterizes conventional romance.

On the other hand, when our boundaries are not abandoned but are instead *expanded to include our partner*, we make possible an exceptionally deep love. When such love's bonding coexists with a naturally succulent, effortlessly mutual erotic chemistry, we can say that we're not just loving, but are *in* love, falling/rising/being in love.

In the presence of such extraordinarily deep communion — shared heart, shared being, shared conditions — there's no need to romanticize, fantasize, or otherwise restrict love.

Me-centered relationships mostly know only romantic love, conditioned love, self-serving love, constituting not much more than egoity trying to meet its needs through relationship. The chemistry may be strong here, but not the friendship. Sex and intimacy are so confused at this stage that they are commonly talked about as if they were but one and the same thing.

In we-centered codependent relationships, romantic love has less of a grip, especially as friendship takes root — but the stronger the friendship, the weaker the chemistry tends to be. In we-centered coindependent relationships, romantic love has all but given up the ghost, friendship between the partners being more important than in earlier stages. And real love? It is becoming increasingly present, but not enough so to consistently inform and enliven the relationship.

In being-centered relationships, awakened love — raw, radiantly alive, passionate, Mystery-embracing yet still profoundly personal love — has fully replaced romantic love.

In such relationships, *the stronger the friendship is, the stronger the chemistry*.

Universal love and the love the partners have for each other intermix much of the time; their love for each other is not just for them, and others near them can usually feel this and benefit from it. Love for partners here is not so much something that they do or practice, as something that they *are*.

And how can we open ourselves more deeply to love?

Practice opening in circumstances that typically would shut you down; practice being grateful when you don't give a damn about being grateful; practice being caring toward yourself when you are beating yourself up for something; practice being caring in the midst of your anger, without, however, shutting it down; practice being compassionate toward yourself when your heart is shut; and don't forget to cut yourself *some* slack in all this, for it's far from a straightforward path, with an abundance of dips and twists and surprises.

When you notice you're not loving your partner, immediately remind yourself — including in the midst of he-said-she-said dramatics — that you *do* love them, letting this reminder play a key guiding role in your communication with them. You may still feel angry, and may still need to express that anger, including heatedly, but such expression will now carry some heart — the very presence of which will likely help our partner to be more receptive to what we're saying.

Remember that love can sometimes be fiery, even fierce, out of sheer compassion. Love is not necessarily just some quiet or peaceful oasis of kindness — though at times it can be — but is also the greatest of passions, knowing no limitation in its depth of feeling.

At first we reach for love; then we love, until we can do so even when we are not being loved; and last, we *become* and *are* love.

Emerging from this is a prayer that goes something like this: *May we be love — and when we are not, may we remember without delay to be love — under all conditions at all times, for the limitless benefit of one and all.*

Chapter Thirty Five

EXCLUSION & INCLUSION IN MATURE MONOGAMY

Mature monogamy excludes in order to include.

Mature monogamy is not just highly exclusive — in narrowing its primary focus to just one other person — but is simultaneously highly *inclusive*, in its choosing to be intimate with *all* of the qualities of both partners, through which intimacy with the qualities of *everyone* is, to whatever degree, also cultivated.

That is, what is felt and known through mature monogamy's radically deep intimacy is far more than just the psychodynamics of its partners. Not only is the One touched through the two, but the Many also.

Something very important to realize about this — great depth blooming out into and coexisting with equally great breadth — is that partners here are not trying to do it; rather, it is an utterly natural and inevitable byproduct of their intimacy.

Mature monogamy's inclusion — an embracing at once expansive and discerning — of the various qualities which characterize *both* partners is much more than just mere tolerance or indiscriminate acceptance, and its awareness of these qualities is more than just mere witnessing or dispassionate observation.

And why? Because of the intimate, stably embodied *coexistence* of its capacity for inclusion and its capacity for awareness.

The more deeply we journey into and embody mature monogamy, the more that awareness and compassionate inclusivity become one. This constitutes the essential spirituality of mature monogamy: *love and awareness functioning as one.*

Mature monogamy's consistently present and well-anchored emphasis on allowing everything — *everything* — to serve the partners' healing and awakening makes it a practice-path of immense power. Nothing is avoided and everything is kept in ego-transcending perspective, with radical intimacy being the context that contains and holds it all. In such intimacy, *connection-with* and *separation-from* — which are both essential developmental processes — come together, joining forces.

Probably the most illuminating and liberating place to practice relational intimacy is in the shared depths — the multidimensional crucible — of mature monogamy. Yes, there are other places offering opportunities for deep intimacy, but none provide mature monogamy's radically intimate peer bond of shared mutuality and experiential possibilities. This is not to devalue other forms of intimacy, but to place them in proper perspective.

A mother and her baby, for example, can share a remarkable intimacy, but there usually is (assuming that both are healthy) not much challenge in it other than that of meeting basic needs — no ego transcendence (since the baby doesn't yet have an ego to transcend), no cocreated articulation of what's happening, no co-journeying through each other's conditioning, no shared appreciation of each other's struggles and mortality, no shared responsibilities to take care of together.

Mature monogamy's inclusivity is not an indiscriminate throwing open of the borders, and so excludes the acting-out of practices that undermine it, such as behaviors, erotic and otherwise, that distract us from our suffering. This means generating and standing behind a no that makes possible a deeper yes.

Though such a "no" may appear to be no more than repression, it is in fact a life-giving renunciation, a wisely informed setting of boundaries that makes possible a deeper freedom.

Immature monogamy entraps; mature monogamy liberates.

Immature monogamy's relational container is a nonexpanding bind, infected with marital shoulds and relief-providing erotic or romantic subplots; by contrast, mature monogamy's relational container is an ever-expanding find, unpolluted by shoulds and neurotic detours.

Immature monogamy fantasizes about being elsewhere, even as it beats itself up for doing so; mature monogamy, on the other hand, is too passionately and stably *here* to even consider being elsewhere, finding through its mutual openings, breakthroughs, and rock-solid integrity an ever-deepening intimacy with the Mystery that is the ground, sky, and all of all that is. The Beloved behind and beyond the beloved.

In the profoundly liberating bondage of mature monogamy, we develop a relationship that cannot but help but be of benefit to all.

Such relationship excludes in order to include; only two are in it, but through their bond, a presence and shared heartfulness is radiated that motivelessly touches and includes all.

Chapter Thirty Six

ATTRACTING OUR BELOVED

(*ESPECIALLY INTENDED FOR THOSE WHO ARE SINGLE*)

So many yearn to be in a genuinely intimate relationship — a relationship that consistently enlivens, deepens, and awakens us — and wonder why they continue to find themselves alone or in relationships that don't really work for them (but which they keep *hoping* will).

So many are having a relationship not with the other — be that other their partner or their hoped-for-beloved — but instead with the other's *potential*. (Such a romancing of tomorrow, such nostalgia for the future, is the essence of hope.)

Some think that all that they have to do to attract their beloved is to wish and intend for that one to somehow show up, but wishing and intending is not enough, no matter how ardently we may believe in our power to manifest what we want.

So how to attract our beloved?

Let's begin by looking at how *not* to attract our beloved.

First of all, let go of thinking that all you have to do is *think* about attracting that one. You may have heard that this is all you need to do, and that if you don't get the results you want, it is simply because you're not putting out the right thoughts in the right way. You may have subscribed to New Age notions about the power of thought to create your reality, especially in the context of the so-called Law of Attraction. Such notions tend to both overemphasize and oversimplify the impact that your thoughts can have, as if by just changing the content and direction of your thoughts you can have whatever you want.

At the same time, though, it is important to recognize the power and impact that our thoughts *do* have, especially when we amplify them, however unwittingly, with our attention. Perhaps what matters most here is not what we are thinking, but what we are *doing* with what we are thinking: Are we identified with our thoughts? Are we allowing them to recruit emotional energy? Are we trying to change them? Are we listening to them uncritically? Are we letting ourselves be controlled by them? Are we aware of them, and if so, to what degree? Are we relating *from* them, or *to* them? And when we are using our thoughts to help manifest something we want, how aware are we of which us — or which level or place in us — is wanting that particular something?

Although directed thought is not all let's-manifest-it wishful thinking, we need to be aware of what is actually motivating it. Drug addicts' directed thought may be very clear and single-pointed when their craving for a fix reaches a certain intensity — there may be a very precise and unwavering focus on the desired object, so that they attract whatever (and whomever) helps fulfill their craving.

Similarly, much of what "we" want is animated and directed not by us, but by our conditioning. We may, for example, seek a partner so as to try to fulfill unmet or badly handled needs from our childhood, and we may romanticize this to such a degree (and perhaps also eroticize it, as described in Chapter 23) that we block ourselves from seeing what is *really* going on. At such times, our conditioning — which we are in all likelihood allowing to refer to itself as us — is running the show, not us.

So it's useful here to shift the focus from where we are going (or wanting to go) to *where we are coming from.* And we cannot simply think or intend our way through this; something deeper is needed, namely a journey into and through our conditioning and its roots.

In short, we don't attract our beloved through thought or intention alone.

And nor do we attract our beloved through manipulation, however tastefully dressed or spiritualized that might be. Presenting ourselves as other than we are means that the other is going to be having a relationship not with us, but with our *self-presentation.* This may "work" for a bit, but sooner or later it wears thin, as the other sees through us, or we simply lose the energy to keep up the façade.

Putting energy into being other than ourselves is ultimately exhausting; the grief which it covers or obscures — the grief over assuming that we, as we are, are not enough — eventually must surface, including through the cracks that inevitably will appear in our self-presentation.

Of course, presenting ourselves as we are is more than just a matter of being an open book; we need to take into account others' openness to really seeing us, as well as their capacity to do so. The entire book does not have to revealed right away; if you give too much, others won't be able to digest and integrate it.

Recently I saw the title of a book that went something like: *How to Seduce Your Beloved.* If you have to seduce that one, what is implied is that he or she wouldn't otherwise be drawn to you. The power — basically power *over* — expressed through the act of seduction (which is little more than eroticized aggression) is simply a confession of an underlying sense of powerlessness; rather than get seductive or otherwise exploitively inclined regarding what we want from another, we would do better to face, explore, and work through the very powerlessness for which our seductiveness is a "solution".

We also won't attract our beloved if we are looking for someone to make us feel whole or better. What we will then attract is someone who has an investment in making us feel whole or better, an investment which probably has its roots in their not being loved (or feeling loved) unless they were busy making someone else, like one of their parents, feel good. Only when we liberate relationship (and everything else!) from the task of making us feel better, will we *truly* feel better.

Something more than positive thinking, intentionality, manipulation, and hope is needed — namely to face, really face, and work through whatever it is in us that's in the way of attracting our beloved. This means not only facing our doubts and self-defeating beliefs, but also facing and working through the originating forces that underlie such doubts and beliefs.

That is, to attract our beloved, we cannot just sit back and think a certain way or do some affirmations or hold a certain intention (which is not to say that such activities are without value) — rather, we have to do some deeper work on ourselves, work that includes and integrates our physical, mental, emotional, social, and spiritual dimensions, so that we'll be sufficiently ready for our beloved. *Ripe.*

Full alignment with what we long for — a relationship that actually works, not later, but *now* — is necessary, and this requires that we not only clearly see our conditioning, but that we also cease letting it run us or refer to itself as us. And we don't do this by somehow getting rid of our conditioning (such eradication being but a fantasy) or rising above it (which is just a form of dissociation), but by relating *to* it instead of *from* it.

Once we have done enough work to be able to see our conditioning for what it is, and to take full responsibility for it when it arises — waking up in the midst of our reactivity, and so on — then we can begin generating potent prayers/invitations for our beloved to come into our life. We are then ready, and we know it, right to our core. Here, thought, intentionality, raw feeling, intuition, and faith all come together to produce a fitting prayer that aligns us with our beloved.

Such prayer may look like wishful thinking, but is not. It may look like it's aimed into the future, but it's not. It may look like it's constructed of hope, but it's not. It is firmly and unshakably rooted in the now, leaving us not leaning into later, but rather deeply settled into the present moment.

Such prayer is a kind of active meditation, conscious and empowering, a clear statement of opening and trust and patience. It is not at all the sort of prayer that is just narcissism or greed or desperation in spiritual garb, asking for stuff (as if from a cosmic catalog or shopping channel that requires only our wishes as payment for its goodies).

Let's now take an in-depth look at prayer and at the levels of prayer, before we continue with the type of prayer best suited for attracting our beloved...

Yes, prayer is desire, but it is the final frontier of desire.

Although prayer may include thought, especially spiritually-oriented thought, it is not primarily an act of mind. It is much more an act of heart. *A divine personal.*

The desire highlighted and presented through mature prayer isn't greedy or desperate for fulfillment, being rooted not in the futurizing of hope, but rather in the here-and-now openness of faith (where hope promises, faith gives; where hope dreams, faith awakens).

Prayer is sacred conversation, even when it is absolutely silent.

In its beginning stages, prayer mostly asks. As it ripens, prayer may still ask, but its primary characteristic is deep, devotional receptivity. So prayer initially has a lot to say, but later on it mostly listens.

(After all, if our beloved-to-be is trying to reach us, why not listen more closely and deeply?)

Ultimately, prayer *becomes* what it is requesting, through bringing us into such deep intimacy with What-Really-Matters that we're no longer significantly separated from the object of our prayer.

Much depends on *who* — or *what* — we assume is hearing our prayers. Let us call the ear we are trying to reach God. If we take God to be a kind of super-parent or cosmic Santa Claus, our prayers will be like those of a child asking for favors. But if we move closer to the other end of the spectrum and take God to be Absolute Nondual Being, our prayers will mostly be communications between wakefulness and Wakefulness.

To whatever degree our attention may be object-oriented (that is, focused on thoughts, feelings, sensations, things, others) — as opposed to being oriented to its source — it still exists in the domain of awareness. When prayer consciously arises and takes shape in the continuum or field — the timeless, infinite field — of awareness, it is *already* in contact with its fruition. (And this our beloved-to-be can arguably feel, through the innate interconnectivity and inseparability of all that is, however difficult that might be to rationally explain.)

That is, what prayer seeks is recognized, at least to some degree, to be *already* found. There is actually no real gap between seeking and sought in bare awareness — it is only in time, only in the manifesting of prayer's requests, that there appears to be a such a gap.

Prayer helps to bridge the unmanifest and the manifest by creating fertile conditions for bringing potentialities to life. Prayer provides templates, sacred and otherwise, for intentionality.

As it matures, prayer's context shifts from petitioning to *gratitude*. Then prayer does not end with a thank you, but *is* a thank you.

It is in the spirit of this that our prayer for our beloved will be most effective. The more we let go of having to have something happen here, the more likely it is to happen. No desperation, no rush, just making haste slowly...

Look at what you have attracted thus far, and find out what it was in you that was the driving force behind such attraction.

See what childhood programming may still be operative in you; see what you saw in the other; see where your charge or excitation (whether positive or negative) was, and still is, in relationship; see which needs you eroticized, and still eroticize; see through the intoxicating dramatics of romance; and *look inside your looking* until your inclination to allow your woundedness to attract your beloved fades to nothing.

When doing your prayer, be very specific and precise when describing the qualities you are looking for. Be thorough. Do the entire list each time you pray (saying each part mindfully and with full feeling), and precede doing so with enough meditation to get you centered, and follow it with enough meditation to settle and reground you.

Be thorough; if you want someone who's taller than you, put that out. If you want someone who is finished with previous relationships, put that out. If you want someone who is committed to being present, put that out. Put it *all* out.

Allow your prayer to expand, deepen, and awaken you. Let your voice, however soft, emanate from your core as much as possible. Let your whole body participate. Be bare-hearted.

Do not ask for anything which you are not prepared to give.

Open yourself to being with someone who is *already* capable of meeting you fully. Don't settle for less.

And remember to remember that your beloved is trying to find *you*. Let yourself feel your beloved's prayers to find and be with you.

Let your longing for your beloved be your primary guide. Separate that longing from other longings, like wanting to feel special or needed.

And remember: You deserve to be *fully* met in relationship. You are worthy of it. Your beloved awaits you. Fill the gap between you and your beloved with love, presence, and integrity.

Feel that gap, that open space, feel your way into it, inhabit it. Feel the already-happening reality of you and your beloved, and make yourself at home in it...

Chapter Thirty Seven

CONCLUSION: TOWARD MATURE MONOGAMY

Everything exists through relationship, and only through relationship. *Everything.* Everything, everyone, everywhere, everywhen, every last bit of it. None of it exists unto itself, truly separate from all the rest of it. None of it!

We are never not in relationship. How could we be? No one and no thing possesses truly independent existence, and therefore cannot really stand apart from everything else. In fact, that very "everything else" is what we depend upon for our very existence.

Every life arises only in the context of relationship.

No matter how far apart we are, we are still connected. No matter how isolated we are, we are still connected. Interconnected and interdependent are we, on every possible scale, outer and inner, regardless of our mental commentary to the contrary.

As sages have long pointed out, there is actually no such thing as a truly separate or truly independent thing or being, but rather only different manifestations or embodiments of the same everpresent reality, all following the meandering arc of their own unique yet ever-contingent leanings, meeting more and more of themselves through each other, however mechanically or unconsciously.

When such encounters become conscious — that is, when interrelatedness itself becomes conscious — real intimacy becomes possible.

Recognizing our inherent unity of being is not the final realization of being human, but rather just the *beginning*. Honoring our unitive nature while simultaneously honoring the imperatives of individuated life is perhaps the core challenge of living a fully human life.

How we differ from each other (and from earlier versions of ourselves) is just as interesting to me as our oneness. Oneness is a given; the rest is not. Evolution — the fact that we *develop* — ensures that this is so.

Objectivity (or the apparent reality of what is exterior) and subjectivity (or the apparent reality of what is interior), both of which are obviously essential to consider when exploring the nature of relationship, are but the presenting surface of something deeper, something that includes both without being reducible to either.

And that something is relationship.

Some say that relationship *is* intersubjectivity (that is, the encounter and interplay of *my* interiority — my feelings, thoughts, perceptions, and so on — with *your* interiority), but there's more to relationship than just your "inner-life/within-ness" and my "inner-life/within-ness" meeting.

We also must take interobjectivity (that is, the encounter and interplay of *my* exteriority — my behavior, physicality, and so on — with *your* exteriority) into account in considering the nature of relationship.

Relationship basically is intersubjectivity *and* interobjectivity operating as *one* process. Inside meeting inside, outside meeting outside, and inside meeting outside, with enough crossover, layering, and hybrid vigor to make things really interesting.

Infuse all this with love and awareness, and the result is intimacy.

In me-centered relationships, intimacy is weak, being almost completely rootless, with an overemphasis on the exteriority of both partners. In we-centered codependent relationships, intimacy is not so anemic, having some rootedness and more emphasis on the interiority of both partners. In we-centered coindependent relationships, intimacy is more stable, with the emphasis on exteriority and interiority being roughly equivalent. In all three cases, however, intimacy remains relatively shallow.

Only when we have reached the stage of being-centered relationship does intimacy go deep and stay deep. Exteriors and interiors are both seen clearly and related to with considerable depth. It is here that the barrier between inside and outside becomes transparent. It is here that love takes firm root. It is here that there is sufficient safety — generated by deep mutual trust — to develop remarkably intimate relationships, relationships in which integrity, compassion, and ecstatic connection are givens. This is the domain of mature monogamy.

We cannot be dropped into such territory (like parachuting tourists), but rather must make our own path toward it, a path that we create and modify with each step we take.

Some steps will take us off our path; our work is to recognize them, explore and cut through whatever thus distracts us, and keep going. There is much work to be done, but the essential work is to keep doing the work.

Along the way, we need to become thoroughly intimate with each relational stage, so that we can recognize it when it surfaces — or when parts of it surface — while we are in a "higher" stage. If we don't recognize it at such times, we will surely regress, perhaps while acting as if we are indeed not thus slipping. Even in well-established being-centered relationships, me-centered tendencies will surface — but when they do, we don't need to get down because of this, but rather only keep such tendencies peripheral to our core of being. We no more need to get rid of our egoity than does the sky need to get rid of its clouds.

Mature monogamy is available *if* we will do the preparatory work. Yes, that work — a true labor of love — is far from easy, but once we get going, we will develop some momentum, and then all we have to do is maintain that momentum (which usually only takes a bit of energy, daily perhaps, but still only a bit).

The path toward mature monogamy is not necessarily a straight one. Like most paths, it has plenty of curves, switchbacks, and rocky sections (and vanishing signposts), asking for a clear eye, courage, flexibility, balance, and steady footing. Each time we lose our balance we are given an opportunity for a deeper balancing. It is an adventure for which we were born, asking everything of us and giving back even more.

We don't leave a relational stage until we've outgrown it, and we don't outgrow it until we've really seen it for what it is. And we will thus see when we have reached a sufficient level of discomfort with where we are. At the me-centered stage, our discomfort has to be very intense for us to ride it into a deeper level of being; at the we-centered codependent stage, things are much the same, but at the we-centered coindependent stage, we don't need such a degree of discomfort to make the needed shift. And at the being-centered stage? Discomfort is taken without delay as an ally, and is used as such, catalyzing our wakefulness and capacity to take needed action.

So as we relationally ripen, we become increasingly comfortable with our discomfort. We also become less disappointed by our disappointments, learning to look upon them with undreaming eyes. And we also stop getting bitter and knotted up about disillusionment, allowing it to sober us and divest us of our illusions, without losing touch with our heart. To share all this in the intimate mutuality that relationship can be is as satisfying as it is liberating.

In a mature or significantly awakened relationship, the two may be profoundly bonded and even spend the majority of their time together, but their togetherness is not cultic. Yes, we don't directly participate in their intimacy, but we nevertheless are touched, opened, and furthered by their unusual closeness, the inner workings of which are openly radiated and communicated. Whatever its privacy, this kind of relationship is not isolated from the rest of Life; rather, it is connected, and willingly connected, to the community-at-large, while maintaining its integrity.

When we're in the presence of such a relationship, such a richly embodied sanctuary of deep intimacy, we tend to feel more open, looser, happier, safer to do deeper work or take needed risks. Mature monogamy feels good to be around. It's that simple.

And mature monogamy also feels good to be in, so good that there is no hankering for more. No dulling familiarity can creep in, nor can anything that lacks integrity — there's just too much connection, love, mutual transparency, and awareness to permit that. Mistakes still happen, but — like the partners' flaws — serve rather than get in the way of the relationship. Their love is too real to have it any other way.

Between immature monogamy and mature monogamy, there's a stretch of often unruly water, wild enough to elude any neat cartography. Jump in, wherever you are. When you hit bottom, push off and surface, then paddle out a bit deeper. Eventually, you will leave the arms of the familiar, and have no bottom to hit, no end to love, no limit to depth. This is the beginning of mature monogamy.

It's well worth the journey. May this book help you to better navigate as you head for deeper waters. May what I have said help deepen your relationship, whether with your partner, yourself, or the world at-large. May you do whatever it takes to make mature monogamy a living reality for yourself. May you find freedom through intimacy.

In love's lucid swoon
You and I are without name
For we then speak a tongue
Not made of words
It's older than meaning
Before and beyond belief
What then shall I call you?
I know your true name
But for it there's no word
Only this naked knowing
That speaks and sings of you
Through all we are and all we do

When navigating the daily grind
Sometimes I call you
By your everyday name
But I know it's not the one for you
For I remember your true name
The one that has no words
But only the pure feel of you
The way you turn your head
And so happily lean into me
As we windingly walk hip to hip
Joined right to the core
In the liberating bondage
That intimacy can be
The signature of your being
Written everywhere in me
Seen and unseen

INDEX

ABOUT THE AUTHOR

My passion is to fuel, illuminate, and support the living of a deeper life, a life of love, integrity, and fully alive awakening. Providing environments (both inner and outer) in which deep healing and transformation can take place is my vocation and privilege.

As I approach my 60th birthday, I notice that I am finding freedom more through intimacy — intimacy not only with my beloved Diane, but also with all that is — than through transcendence. There is a deeply satisfying joy for me in passing on what I have learned, especially through my integral psychotherapy apprenticeship programs and the couples intensives that I do with Diane.

Since 1977 I've worked as a psychotherapist (I have a Ph.D. in Psychology), group leader, bodyworker, and teacher of spiritual deepening practices, creatively integrating the physical, mental, emotional, and spiritual in my practice. Most weekends these days I'm leading groups or trainings.

Evolving in fitting parallel with this has been my writing, which is as much a passion for me as facilitating deep groupwork. I've authored eight books, including *Divine Dynamite* and *Darkness Shining Wild.* My essays have appeared in magazines ranging from *Magical Blend* to the *Journal of Transpersonal Psychology*, as well as in several anthologies. And running rampant through all my writing is my poetry, keeping my prose on its toes.

If you would like to find out more about my work and writings, visit **www.RobertMasters.com**. While there, you can, if you wish, view my blog and subscribe to my free newsletter (*The Crucible of Awakening*).

O BREATHE US DEEP

Diane & Robert's CD

One day in late March 2005, I came across the website of Robert Augustus Masters, an author and psychotherapist from Vancouver, and there began looking at descriptions of his books. I noticed that he also posted his poetry on his site; when I read his poems, particularly one called Sacred Hymn, I literally gasped and touched my heart. With total certainty, I realized that I knew the music for these "poems," which I felt were meant to be lyrics for songs.

And so I emailed him to ask if he would allow me to try composing music for them, and he consented. After 3 weeks of talking on the phone, consulting about the songs and having many conversations about everything else imaginable, Robert came to where I was living in California to meet me and hear Sacred Hymn during a concert I was giving. Our connection was extremely easy, deep, and natural right from the start. That was the beginning of our co-creative relationship, working partnership, and, since April 2, 2006, our marriage!

The lyrics for each song on the CD are Robert's, and the music is mine, but the entire CD is ours to share. May you hear it in the spirit in which it was created.

Much has been birthed out of the depths of our being together, including not only this our first CD and Robert's new book on mature monogamy, but also an abundance of deep work with others, primarily through groupwork and training programs that blend psychotherapy, bodywork, and spiritual deepening practices (as described on Robert's website: http://www.robertmasters.com). It feels as if our relationship cannot get any deeper, but it does, and for this we both feel profoundly grateful. This CD is but one expression of that gratitude.

~ Diane Bardwell Masters

The songs are: *Sacred Hymn*
O Breathe Us Deep
Look For Me
Take Me to the Bottom of Your Pain
I Come to You
This the Open Ground
And Again
Last Sigh of a Vagabond Wave

To hear a sound clip of each, and to see the lyrics, click on the Music button at www.RobertMasters.com.

To purchase, click on the Store button at www.RobertMasters.com.

My life sings and bleeds in colors bare and bright
Riding waves of shattered moon through the night
Nothing is moving yet everything's in motion
Only broken waves will ever know the ocean

DIVINE DYNAMITE
(Revised Edition)

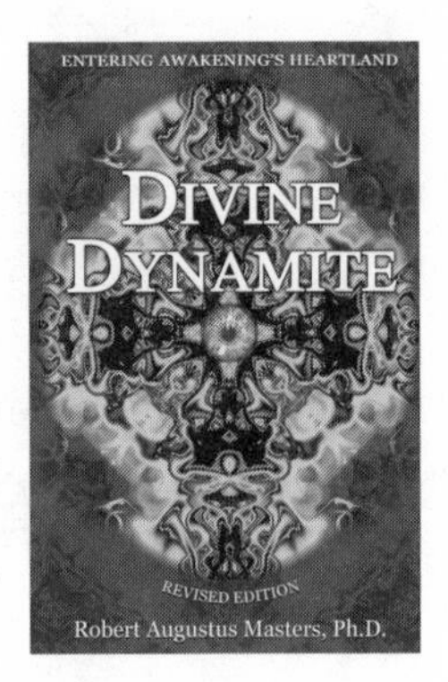

Forty-nine essays that explore and illuminate the promises, perils, and terrain of the awakening process, providing steppingstones and navigational savvy for the inevitably slippery slopes of personal, transpersonal, and interpersonal evolution.

"*Divine Dynamite* is just what it says it is — a sacred explosion! Masters transforms the spiritual landscape with the mind-bending freshness of his prose. With the dexterity of the true master, he shatters complacency and razes the familiar with startling beauty. This book embodies the constantly novel surprise that is the heart of true realization."

Jenny Wade, Ph.D., author of TRANSCENDENT SEX

"Don't expect linearity or logic from *Divine Dynamite*; take satisfaction in being provoked and having your ordinary understanding of reality stretched and transformed.....A splendid book!"

Stanley Krippner, Ph.D., co-author of THE MYTHIC PATH

"This is such a powerful book! Written on the fire that melds the single heart into the underlying alchemical explosion that rises through the spine of those surrended into the great unknowing, the original fire from which we were forged. Well done!"

Stephen Levine, author of HEALING INTO LIFE & DEATH and A YEAR TO LIVE

AVAILABLE IN BOOKSTORES OR FROM AMAZON.COM

FREEDOM THROUGH INTIMACY

Transformational Intensives For Couples

with

ROBERT MASTERS & DIANE BARDWELL

Deeply embodied and highly effective integral work for couples who (1) want a more conscious, loving, and liberating relationship with each other, and (2) are ready to work through whatever's in the way.

Individual work will be given as much emphasis as couples work, using a dynamic, spontaneously structured approach that creatively mixes psychotherapy, bodywork, dream exploration, spiritual disciplines, and couples practices.

Intensives are small and intimate, being limited to five couples only, so that there is plenty of time for fittingly deep work for each participant and couple.

For more information, visit **www.RobertMasters.com** and click on Groupwork.

If you are interested in having Robert and Diane bring their couples work to your area, contact **info@RobertMasters.com**.